Aurea Vidyā Collection

———— 1 ————

*For a complete List of Titles, see page 221.

THE THREEFOLD PATHWAY OF FIRE

This book was originally published in Italian
as, Raphael, *La Triplice Via del Fuoco*, Pensieri che vibrano
Edizioni Āśram Vidyā, Rome

First published in English in 2000 by
Aurea Vidyā.
39 West 88th Street, New York, N.Y. 10024, U.S.A.
www.vidya-ashramvidyaorder.org

© Āśram Vidyā 1986
 Third Edition 2009
 English Translation ©Āśram Vidyā 2000

Set in font © Vidyā 11/13 points by Aurea Vidyā

Printed and bound by Lightning Source Inc. at locations in the
U.S.A. and the U.K., as shown on the last page.

ISBN 10: 1-931406-00-6
ISBN 13: 978-1-931406-00-0
Library of Congress Control Number: 2001119962

On the Cover: "Philosophy"
             Nathan David, Bronze plate.

RAPHAEL

(Āśram Vidyā Order)

THE THREEFOLD
PATHWAY OF FIRE

Thoughts that Vibrate
for an alchemical, æsthetical and metaphysical ascesis

AUREA VIDYĀ

«'Oh Yama, you who know the Fire that leads to Heaven, reveal it to me who am full of faith'.

'I will teach you that Fire, oh Naciketas, that will raise you up to Heaven. Know that Fire is the means by which to attain infinite worlds; It is their very foundation and is hidden in a secret place'.

He then revealed to him that Fire, the source of the world».

(Kaṭha Upaniṣad: I, I, 13-15)

TABLE OF CONTENTS

INTRODUCTION

The "Pathway of Fire" by Raphael is the *operative means* by which one can lead light up the Fire, to master and direct the Fire and the solution of that very Fire.

Following the Initiatory Tradition, Raphael expounds this process of realization in three operative ways, in order to suit each person's qualifications:

I Realization according to Alchemy
(Section One, Chapter I)

II Realization according to Love of Beauty
(Section One, Chapter II)

III Realization according to Traditional Metaphysics
(Section One, Chapter III)

I. What does Raphael mean by Alchemy?

The *transmutation* of "lead" into shining and radiant Gold, the transmutation of all our individualized psycho-physical *powers* into Universal Powers; this implies a profound *rectification* and distillation of our individualized earthly fire, so as to turn it into a Fire able to penetrate, illumine and resolve all things.

When the individual, having isolated himself in the extreme periphery of the cosmos-life returns to the Polar Center, through

an act of consciousness revolution, conversion and rectification, he ceases to be a mere individual-being at the mercy of
karma's currents and resolves himself in the Universal Being
(*Adam Kadmon*), in order to stabilize himself within his own
Heart and thus in the Heart of everything.

In order to achieve awareness of this Awakening, the disciples have to experience the phases of the *Opus* on their own,
first detaching themselves from all social habits which are the
expression of those who "allow themselves to be lived" rather
than *live*. Suitable and opportune aid comes to the disciples
who know how to knock. But it must be pointed out to
them that Alchemy, like any other Pathway to Realization,
is not a theoretical philosophy with an end onto itself, but a
Philosophy of death-rebirth, a Philosophy which teaches how
to die while living. This means achieving a total revolution
in one's way of thinking, feeling and acting.

Often individuals mentally embrace a philosophy and
barely give themselves the time to assimilate it before they
begin teaching and trying to convert others to it. To speak of
Alchemy or of Hermetism is not very difficult, but it is difficult to live by it, *apply* it to oneself, and not to others first.

Whoever is digging his own "grave" has no time to waste
on extroversion, chatting or being enthralled by the "social
object".

In his synthetic alchemical aphorisms, Raphael proposes
four phases which obviously coincide with those of Traditional
Alchemy:

1. Rectification of the Fires

2. Fixation of the Mercury-Fire

3. Separation of the Rectified Mercury-Fire

4. Conjunction with the Sulphur-Fire.

Raphael's expression is not discursive because his intention is not that of fostering people's erudition but of indicating to those who are ready a precise consciential position to be realized. Thus, these aphorisms may disappoint the majority, but may prove precious to those few who, rather than thinking to Be, *want* to Be.

II. The Second Chapter of the First Section is dedicated to Realization by means of Love of Beauty. This way is for those who are *sensitive* toward "Transcendental Æsthetics" meant as Harmony-Accord with the intelligible world. According to Coomaraswamy, *Brahman* or the Supreme Being may be conceived of as Beauty, Truth or Perfection, depending on whether we see it from an æsthetic, epistemological or ethical point of view.

Art is an expression of Beauty. Science, in a broad sense, is an expression of truth, ethics of Perfection; while the *Philosophia Perennis* or traditional metaphysics embraces them all. This shows that the three expressions are a unit: Beauty contains Truth and Perfection, Truth contains Beauty and Perfection, while Perfection cannot but contain Beauty and Truth.

The theory of Traditional Art taken as a the whole – as Coomaraswamy holds in his *The Transformation of Nature in Art* – is based on the following fundamental concepts:

1) The æsthetic experience is an inscrutable ecstasy in itself, but insofar as it may be defined, it is the delight of reason.

2) The work of art, acting as a stimulation to the spirit to free itself from the ties of vision, is produced and has meaning on condition that it aims at specific goals. Heaven and earth are merged in the analogy of art which leads sen-

sation toward the sphere of the intelligible and tends toward that ultimate perfection where he who contemplates sees all things reflected in himself.

The greatest masterpiece which the individual can create is that of making himself "beautiful" in imitation of the archetype of Divine Beauty (Transcendental Æsthetics).

«To any vision must be brought an eye adapted to what is to be seen, and having some likeness to it. Never did eye see the sun unless it had first become sun-like, and never can the Soul have vision of the First Beauty unless it is itself be beautiful.

Therefore, first let each who cares to see God and Beauty become godlike and beautiful».

«Beauty addresses itself chiefly to sight; but there is a beauty in the hearing too, as in certain combinations of words and in all kinds of music... and minds that lift themselves above the realm of sense to a higher order are aware of beauty in the conduct of life, in actions, in character, in the pursuits of the intellect; and then there is the beauty of the virtues. What loftier beauty there may be, yet, our argument will bring to light».

«But there is a transcendent Beauty. In the sense-bound life we are no longer granted to know it, but the Soul, taking no help from the sensory organs, sees and proclaims it. To the vision of these we must rise and contemplate, leaving sense to its own low place»[1].

---

[1] Plotinus, *Enneads*, I, 6: 9, 1, 4, translated by Stephen MacKenna, Larson Publications, Burdett, NY, U.S.A. (Minor revisions added).

The Fire of Love distracts thought from sensible things and raises the Soul up to intelligible things. Love of Beauty in itself turns the gaze away from sensory forms which are only reflections, shadows, imperfect imitations of Beauty.

«Beauty which is also the Good, must be posed as the first: directly deriving from this Good is the Spirit which is pre-eminently the manifestation of Beauty; through the Spirit the Soul is made beautiful. The beauty in things of a lower order – actions and pursuits for instance – comes by operation of the molding Soul which is also the author of the beauty found in the world of sense. For the soul, a divine thing, a fragment as it were of Beauty, makes beautiful to the fullness of their capacity all things that it grasps and molds»[1].

This transcendent Beauty may be realized by opening up the inner *sight*, *hearing* and *touch* so as to see, hear and perceive vital quality-essences rather than quantity-forms. The musician must be able to *appreciate*, by means of his own particular sensitivity toward accord, intelligible or sacred Harmony, just as the lover must find in the Beloved an accord with the universal symphony of Love.

If the five senses have *appreciated* the beauty of the sensible world, gradually they must give way to other "senses" capable of perceiving and appreciating the Beauty of the intelligible world, compared to which the sensible one is but a pale reflection. The changing things of the sensory dimension are beautiful insofar as they participate, in a more or less perfect way, in the Beauty of the Eternal Ideas upon the intelligible plane.

---

[1] *Ibid*, I, 6: 6. .

The traditional pathway of Realization proposed by Raphael in the second chapter of this book as well as in other books[1], is difficult because one must have a particular *sensitivity* toward Accord-Harmony which is not of a strictly sensorial-emotional nature.

III. The third chapter is dedicated to the "Metaphysical Pathway". This is useful for those who, abandoning the limited, discursive mind, wish to enter the realm of pure Intellection (*Noûs*). In this dimension the two previous pathways merge because in the One-without-a-second all quantities (number) and all qualities (tone) are resolved.

What may cause a deviation from the first pathway is impurity of heart, that is, inadequate rectification of powers; what may cause a deviation from the second pathway is a sense of appropriation directed toward the world of forms; and what may cause a deviation from the third pathway is a selective, analytical and projecting mind that blocks the way to pure Intellectuality which alone can offer "Knowledge of Identity", where the subject and the object of knowledge disappear.

We have three "senses": the bodily, through which we discover the material world; the rational, through which we get to know deep inside ourselves; the contemplative through which we get to know the divine world or the world of the pure intelligible.

When the thirst to reveal the Truth, Beauty and divine Will exists, these pathways may be followed without danger, and the Greater Life certainly offers all the opportunities that one may need.

---

[2] See Raphael, *Initiation into the Philosophy of Plato*, the chapter dedicated to the "Ascension of the Philosophical Eros". Aurea Vidyā. New York..

The Chapters in Section Two address specific points of ascetic orientation; they are meant to aid and complement the three chapters in Section One. The Chapter "Superimposition" concerns and complements the Third Chapter; "Non-desire" and "The empirical ego" the First Chapter. The other ones are auxiliary to all three.

Aurea Vidyā

SECTION ONE

I

FIRE OF LIFE

Realization according to Alchemy

1. If you raise your eyes to heaven you only see the splendor of Fire. If you turn your eyes toward the earth you only see condensed Fire. If you look within yourself you only see whirlpools of liquid Fire.

2. We can observe the development of a star in terms of Fire-Light. The greater or lesser intensity of its fire reveals its existential state. Thus, we can observe the development of an individual in terms of intensity of Fire-Light and of radiance.

3. Manifestation is a rainbow of light, a combination of Fires responding to the focal note of Being.

A body-form-volume is a synthesis of condensed or radiant Fires which express focal qualities.

4. «Hermes says that in order to obtain marvelous effects fire and earth are sufficient, the former being active, the latter receptive. According to Dionysus, Fire exists in every thing, for every thing, while it is not in any one thing. It exists in itself without accompanying matter upon which it exercises its action and through which it reveals itself and so it illuminates everything, although remaining invisible and occult. It is invisible, boundless an by its very nature capable of action, mobile and capable of communicating to all who approach it. It renews strength and preserves nature and is incomprehensible on account of its splendor... able to move as soon as it is moved. Fire comprehends all the other elements while

remaining hidden and without needing them. By its very nature fire is able to grow and transmit its greatness to the objects that it fills with itself... it reduces matter... it does not diminish however abundantly it concedes itself»[1].

5. In the *Corpus Hermeticum* mention is made of a "Robe of Fire" possessed by the spirit, of which a mere particle would suffice to destroy the earth. Flamel states: «Fire is generated and nourished by Fire and is the Child of Fire, therefore it needs to return to Fire in order not to fear Fire»[2].

6. «It (nature) knows itself and I know it. I have contemplated the light that is in it and I have demonstrated it in the microcosm and found it again in the macrocosm»[3].

7. *Kuṇḍalinī* which rests at the base of the spine (*mūlā-dhāra cakra*), is the non-vulgar Fire which must be raised to heaven to join Śiva's Fire. Remember as and from now that our mysterious Fire (*salamander*), heavenly Light, is to be found in your "cave"; without this Fire, hidden also in the bowels of Aries, no operation is possible.

8. «'Oh Yama, you who know the Fire which leads to Heaven, reveal it to me who am full of faith'.

'I will teach you that Fire, oh Naciketas, that will raise you up to Heaven. Know that Fire is the means by which to

---

[1] H. Cornelius Agrippa: *De occulta philosophia*, I, V.

[2] N. Flamel, *Le Désire désiré*, VI.

[3] Paracelsus, *Thesaurus Thesaurorum Alchimistorum*.

attain infinite worlds; It is their very foundation and is hidden in a secret place'.

He then revealed to him that Fire, the source of the world»[1].

9. Within you, rainbows of color intertwine: some lights shine revolving about themselves; other lights, like darting-flames, mix with the vital fire that surrounds you. What a universe of Fire!

10. Your instinct is a jet of fire trying to resolve itself, to manifest itself; your emotion-passion is a liquid fire made of joy or mortification; your mind is a fire that molds – either harmoniously or disharmoniously – your destiny.

When you think, you are ākāśic Fire; when you express an emotion-sentiment you are solar Fire; when you explode in an instinct you are electric Fire.

11. When you gaze, rays of fire flash from your eyes, when you move flames of fire dart from your body and when you rest fire envelops you.

12. Cinders of elements... Ardor of cosmoses...
Flames of earth, of pollen, of flesh.
Fires of pure atoms that come, disappear,
return in an unceasing whirlwind.
Oh Life: eternity and instant!
Oh Life: fire and flames of accord!

13. The single entity, sooner or later, is bound to render itself radiant, just as in the mineral world every element,

---

[1] *Kaṭha Upaniṣad*: I, I, 13-15, in, *Upaniṣad*, Edited by Raphael. Bompiani. Milan. (Italian Edition).

sooner or later, becomes radioactive. To realize this passage, from coagulation to solution, from condensation to radiance, one must learn the Art.

The Art is what teaches the value of being able to "die" like true Philosophers, the Beauty of making oneself commensurable with radiance.

14. Mass, which is made of condensed Fires, must become pure Energy, radiant Light-Fire, so that the entity may conquer immortality.

Science has demonstrated that "mass" may be converted into radiant "energy" and vice versa. Perennial and sacred Art has taught us from time immemorial how to live this truth. Whoever approaches Art approaches Fire, and Fire may imprison, render mortal or concede freedom and immortality.

15. If you study your condensed Fires – egocentric psycho-physiological reactions – you will realize how metallic, reductive and one-sided they have made you. Are you amazed to see your Gold buried in a cave of lead?

The "Pathway of Fire" tells you that you can transmute your lead into Gold: the "future" is in your hands, radiance is within you and only you can release it and make it manifest.

16. The "Pathway of Fire" can be divided into three parts:

1. *The Pathway of Alchemy* (Fire of Life)

2. *The Pathway of Beauty* (All-pervading Fire)

3. *The Metaphysical Pathway* (Colorless Fire).

The first Pathway in turn is made up of four phases:

a) Rectification of the Fires

b) Fixation of the Fire-Mercury

b) Separation of the Rectified Fire-Mercury

d) Conjunction of mercurial Fire with noumenal Fire (Sulphur)

17. The comprehension of your inner Fires reveals to you the synthesis of your life; the comprehension of Universal Fires reveals to you the Fire of Being; identity with the Essence of Fire reveals to you the Supreme Non-Manifest Reality.

18. We may speak of Light-Fire, but also of Sound. Do not think that they are the sound of a musical instrument or mere wood fire, although these are its expressive symbols. The "Pathway of Fire" speaks to you in terms of Fire-Light and Sound. «Sound is Fire which vibrates and darts...».

The "Pathway of Fire" is not written in books, nor is it charted on paper because it is not the fruit of erudition.

The "Pathway of Fire" is born, grows and resolves itself in creative living; it is matured through direct experience and awareness of being ($\odot$).

Knowing, experiencing and living are the three sparks of the "Pathway of Fire".

Ardor, daring and ascending are the foundations of the "Pathway of Fire".

19. The "Pathway of Fire" reveals the Art of harmonious living, the Beauty of being a unity or a link in the Universal chain of Being and the Bliss of discovering oneself to be in the likeness of Essence.

20. To know Fire in its manifold expressions is to possess its Power; but while this makes slaves of the fearful, it grants freedom to the strong. The "Pathway of Fire" is not for the weak.

21. In your "furnace" are comprehended Fire, the genesis of Fire, the pathway that leads to knowledge of Fire and the solution of Fire itself.

If you venture outside of yourself, you will find only the reverberation or the reflection of the true Fire. You cannot practice the Art if you do not recognize within yourself the different principles of Fire. Know that your "vessel" holds the Philosophic Fire which animates and modifies the elements; it is a Spiritual Fire capable of penetrating the substance of our Teaching, of moving it, contracting or dilating it and carrying into act what it possesses at the potential level.

22. Be the Lord of your Temple; may the powers of Fire that abide in it not bite you, making you a slave. Learn the Art of the divine operation that makes you master of the Fires and forger of destinies.

This is the "Pathway of Fire".

23. The "Pathway of Fire" is a total dissolution of supports. All supports, fed by individualised Fire, are abandoned for the sole and unutterable support which is the "Pathway of Fire". But the "Pathway of Fire" is the ineffable support that *self-resolves* into non-support.

24. An initiatory Pathway is for the very few. The majority thirst for mystery, for material or psychic powers; they want to adapt to profane life so they need psychological comfort and

commiseration. The majority wish to perpetuate their own incompleteness; they love to accentuate worldly or heavenly values and to "blow their trumpets" in the market place. The true Philosophers of the Art do not love the market place or fashionable circles and they are not noisy because they are profoundly meditative as they cannot afford to waste their energies. Whoever is trying "to die while living" cannot afford distractions, commiseration or to listen to nonsense and trifles. Every being must learn to find its own place, must learn to fulfill its own *dharma*.

25. There is an esoteric and an exoteric way. Many are suited to the latter, and to help them they have available a wealth of written material on the subject. Although the esoteric or initiatory way may be written about, it cannot be described; although it may be spoken of, it cannot be conceptualized.

26. If you are asked to speak, answer: give me the Fire of Knowledge.

If you are asked to love, answer: give me the Fire of Love.

If you are asked to relieve someone of a burden, answer: give me the Fire of Power.

The "Pathway of Fire" is for those who want above all to fill their own satchels.

One cannot give what one does not possess.

The majority hope to give what they have not. The majority hope to give without possessing. The empirical ego lives and perpetuates itself in a state of illusion.

27. Do not try to "transform" others; transform yourself. Only your completion can render complete the vital space that surrounds you.

The "Pathway of Fire" means resolving oneself so as to resolve.

28. Do not think that the "Pathway of Fire" consists in studying the science of the stars, healing, magic and the like (even though everything, at its own level, is at its proper place). The Way to Immortality cannot be obtained by begging for a few crumbs at the table of phenomenal erudition, searching for some modest, spectacular psychic power or for some medal or other, conferred by a "spiritual" or pseudo-esoteric organization, to hang upon a wall in order to boost the pride of your begging ego.

The Way to Immortality is revealed to those who, with Dignity, are able "to die" standing up.

29. The phenomenal ego is always looking for Harmony because, obviously, it cannot find it within itself. But when the ego is given a few notes of the Art, has objections and expects to impose its own art which is made of incompleteness. The ego – mere shadow projected by the mind – is swept away by irrational desire and separative will, self-gratification and physical and psychological independence, but it is always obliged to beg for something, selling itself even at a very low price.

The "Pathway of Fire" erects the Temple of the immortal Self upon the ashes of the empirical self.

30. Every desire is something incomplete and stems from a "lack", from dissatisfaction, sensory instability and from an unresolved subconsciousness. Desire fleetingly gratifies and soothes a mind unable to comprehend. Desire is mere escape from one's own incompleteness. One desires because one is not.

The "Pathway of Fire" extinguishes the thirst for extroverted desire and the being finds itself in all-inclusive fullness.

31. You are a flame of the one all-pervading Fire. You are in conflict and live in the solitude of the ego because you consider yourself a little flame separated from its Source.

The "Pathway of Fire" awakens you to the recognition of the fact that you are an integral part of Universal or Radiant Fire. Then it tries to direct your "heat" and your "ardor" toward the heart of your true and innermost Being and finally, It gives you wings to fly toward the Beauty of noumenal Fire.

32. Your sensorial ego, urged by the alchemical Dragon, forced you to beg for physical and psychological love and tricked you into believing that you could love, but it has always loved itself. In order to perpetuate itself the ego needs reassuring alibis. It has given you the hope of perfection and Harmony but you often had to crumble under the hammer of metaphysical ignorance. Suffering, if properly comprehended, is a research tool of the Pathway of Harmony.

33. Haste is not for those who wish to learn the Art of alchemical Harmony. Often the conflicting ego asks: what must I do? The Soul answers: go to school to learn the Art.

The egocentric mind is anxious to hurry and to quench its thirst for curiosity, especially when chased by the tiger of suffering, but the Art cannot be learnt by mere curiosity or in a few hours.

34. To love the Art means, first of all, to love Life; it means being prepared to give to space the Beauty of Harmony; it means being aware of the fact that the surest and

most precious Gold is to be found in the innermost recesses of one's own Being.

35. To believe that conflict, pain, violence and ignorance, etc., are absolute, natural and indisputable data is the gravest of errors. In fact, by firmly believing in this false concept, the individual ends up falling back more and more upon himself, becoming agnostic and cynical and being convinced that "life is like that".

Many uphold similar one-sided points of view, thus pointing toward psychological suicide.

The "Pathway of Fire" is the operative Way to overcome this suicidal fallacy.

36. Why are you sad if you live in a state of conflict? Why do you cry over your misfortunes? Why do you suffer on account of your ignorance? Why do you grow so distressed over your own death? Life offers ignorance and knowledge, hate and love, conflict and joy, death and immortality. Depending on where you direct your steps you may come across either one or the other of these modes of expression.

37. Fulcanelli states that «As long as Fire shall last, man will be able to use his industrious talents to mold the things that surround him and, thanks to this fiery tool, he will be able to bend them to his will, shape them and subject them to his needs. As long as Fire shall last, man will be in direct contact with God and the creature will thus know his Maker better... Fire surrounds us and bathes us on all sides... we feel it acting in us during the whole period of our earthly existence. Our birth is the result of its incarnation; our life

is the outcome of its dynamic movement and our death the result of its disappearance»[1].

38. The "Pathway of Fire" is not a course at the end of which one receives a degree. The Pathway is forged by the power of ascesis of our consciousness, by the transfiguration of individuality. A truly Realized person is the full bloom of generations, the peak of a state to which many individuals have cooperated either consciously or unconsciously. Upon the plane of life-relation no one should proclaim himself self-sufficient.

39. Discernment, intelligent reflection, the study of sacred texts and the company of the great Sages are the essential bases of spiritual ascesis. Psychological willingness and that of consciousness are the key to open the doors of the impossible.

40. Perhaps your hope is that of enriching your individuality more and more by means of power, money or other things.

I dare say that the "Pathway of Fire" is not meant to make men but Gods. Know that Immortality can be obtained from the ashes of your "vulgar compound", while you will be able to obtain Eternity, or the absence of time-space-cause, from the death-solution of any state, be it human or divine. When Fire has devoured the entire fire, you will reveal yourself as imperishable Essence of Fire.

---

[1] Fulcanelli, *Le dimore filosofali*. Vol. II, Ch. XI Edizioni Mediterranee, Roma. (Italian edition).

Rectification of the Common Fires (Nigredo)
and
Fixation of the Philosophical Mercury

41. Collect what is scattered in that place without joy, rectify the inner fault and fly toward the Fire of fullness.

42. Sit down, set your mind at rest and meditate deeply *upon that* which urges you to think, to plan thing-events and to accumulate arrogance, fame, importance (in the eyes of others), vanity, material and scholarly wealth, etc.

Follow the energy of pleasure or pain and observe all as you might observe an external object that stands before you.

Be constant in the practice of *observation* for days, months or years.

While observing be a detached "observer", the "point at the center of the sun" in your own lunar ebb and tide. You must be like the sun (☉) which rotates on its own axis; you must not let yourself be carried away by the titanic powers that exist within your psychic space or within your "hermetic vessel". Be *neutral consciousness*, yet positive.

If you persist, your re-conquered "solar power" will resolve the lunar forces that constrain you until they are finally dissolved.

43. Rather than toward the instrument of contact (☖) of the mercurial Center (☿), observation must be directed toward your "reactions" or requests that arise in you after a given

stimulus. Observe, for instance, how the pleasure-energy of gluttony is born, how it gushes up to the conscious level and how it ripens into objective expressions.

Observe the way the energy of sexual fire rises, how it takes hold of you, how it compels you and how it exhausts you.

Observe how the fire of self-assertion or of vanity etc., arises, matures and determines you.

Observe the "greed" and "thirst" for individualized experiences.

In pure observation the mental fire must be silent and its rays must be resolved; discursiveness prevents pure observation. Thought "opens", so seal your door hermetically.

If you listen to a piece of music, you must listen to it without any discursive intrusion, otherwise you are not listening. Be attentive, deeply attentive to the *present moment.*

Nor must you lose yourself in the object being observed: you must simply be *conscious* of the event and of the alchemical process. You must – above all – have the courage to observe in a *direct* way, and not indirectly through the senses, those fleeting fires that you have lit and fed within yourself. This is what the "descent into hell" (*katàbasis*)[1] consists of. It is the *Nigredo* or "Black *Opus*". Our "seed" must be interred and "die" to be born again into a new life.

Before carrying out total "separation", you must rectify the "substance", weighed down and turned into lead by the coagulation of qualified powers, and you must "fix" the mercurial consciousness-Center or mercurial Fire.

Know that the preliminary phases are the most important although often underestimated and without which one arrives at the opening of the Door without sufficient Dignity.

---

[1] See, Ch. VII, Orphic Ascesis, in, Raphael, *Orphism and the Initiatory Tradition*, Aurea Vidyā, New York.

If you observe and think that you may be overpowered by the bite of the "Scaly Dragon" do not proceed any further; recognize the fact that you are not ready. To continue the *Opus* would mean letting yourself be invaded by the chaotic multitude of the Dragon's projections. In order to begin extracting Gold from within your own "Cave" there must be at least some Solarity, without which the *Opus* would certainly lead to serious consequences.

On the other hand the Dragon must be faced because that is the starting point of the *Opus*; in it the alchemical or philosophical materials are contained in a potential state.

44. If you know how "to observe" you will notice that the fleeting fires crystallized, lit and fed by the grindstone of becoming, diminish in strength and in driving power; at the same time you will experience the *stabilizing* or the fixing of the mercurial Fire. Remember that the alchemical phases are not divided or separate, but they overlap.

In order to observe, you must place yourself at the proper focal distance from the object to be observed: if it is too far away it cannot be seen and if it is too close the content is out of focus. This operation is called the "balancing" of the sun-center or mercurial Fire which on the one hand must wrench itself away from identification with the fleeting fires and must separate and free itself from the scales of the "Dragon", while on the other it must find its stability and *fixity* in order to observe, without being overpowered by the movements of the metal compounds and by the dynamism of the crystallized psychic contents.

In fact, as I have already mentioned to you, there are some dangers involved in carrying out this phase: the "infernal", "titanic" state is inhabited by coagulated "entities" qualified in various ways. Some of these "entities" might appear before your *observing consciousness* which, not being stable and fixed in itself, might let itself be absorbed, believing itself to be what it is not. The "entity" may be positive or negative, may be an image of the Messiah or a warrior or the spirit of a caste; it may even be the very power of the organic substance, so that your consciousness feels as if it were a gigantic organic body; and so on. Be careful and remain placid and serene, continue to be *present* and the *impassive* and self-possessed observer you are. You *are not* the observed product even if such a product may offer tempting prospects of success. Know, however, that the "fixity" of the volatile is granted to you by the heavy and slow lead-Saturn. «Happy is he, exclaims Philaletes, who is able to greet this slow-moving planet»[1].

45. Total "separation" may occur when the fleeting fires have been quenched; to separate before *rectifying* or *fixing* means entering the world of *shadows* rather than that of the Gods.

The "matter" of the *Opus* must first be cleansed, washed, whitened or rectified. The Gold cannot be extracted because the substance is weighed down by the lead element. This operation may be considered as a "Calcination" because the substance submitted to the action of Fire loses its impure and combustible parts.

46. Whoever gathers and absorbs himself in the mercurial focal Pole does not reach out any more toward exterior and profane events.

Whoever can wear down the outward-going movement of the powers flows back into the integral primordial state and tastes the sulphureous joy of Harmony.

---

[1] I. Philaletes, *Introitus apertus ad occlusum Regis Palatium*, XXII

47. The present position of your consciousness may appear as follows:

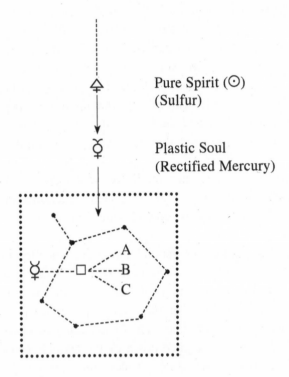

♀ = Vulgar Mercury

□ = Mercurial Center or mercurial Fire under the lunar influence (☽)

A = Mental body

B = Emotional body, Sentiment

C = Instinctive or vital-physical body

• = Contents or the crystallized powers impelled by the irrational strength of the "Scaly Dragon" which must be observed and dissolved.

The mercurial Center (☿) is held down by the power of the fleeting fires and by the overwhelming strength of the mental, emotional and instinctive bodies. The identification and assimilation of the mercurial solar Center with the mother-substance has placed you in a constrained and lunar position. This is the "fall": you who are Immortal discover yourself to be, apparently, mortal. Sulphur and Mercury are interred in the philosophical sepulcher; they must be awakened by "grinding" the bodily salt to the point of putrefaction by means of the projection of the First Fire. The Philosophical Mercury holds the key to this process. Pure Spirit (*Noûs*), says Orpheus, has locked itself up in a *tomb*; it must be freed, therefore, by the fire of the *Psyché*-soul or Philosophical Mercury.

48. Wake up! Arise! Be full of hope. Do not crystallize yourself in false sophisms, do not weigh down your heart which is yearning for perfection. Spread the wings of Knowledge-Awareness, light the radiant mercurial Fire and fly toward Harmony and Beauty which will shatter conflict and ignorance.

49. Daring stems from the awareness of being and from the stupendous vision that you are not alone. Break the circle that binds you in fear and soar into the Movement that overcomes solitude and death.

50. Why follow the shattering pathway of noise? Why hide the doors of Heaven? Steep yourself in silence and let Life reveal the Harmony of the spheres.

51. Metaphysical ignorance has covered you with gaping wounds. What are you doing? Are you trying to heal yourself with the treacherous remedy of pleasure? You have not understood.

52. Rectification or purification is fulmination which awakens the central mercurial Fire that, in turn, destroys every vile and imperfect element within the bodily Temple until it strikes the phantom operating in the sphere of change. And then you will witness the flight of the raven. Remember that the "philosophical Fire is that with which the Philosophers wash the substance"; I.N.R.I. (*Igne Natura Renovatur Integra*): Fire renews all things.

53. Blessed is he who builds his "tomb" with his own hands. The death of the Wise is not the death of those who ignore the Art.

54. Bury the perishable body together with the arsenical phantom of the old Dragon, catch the invincible and darting Body, that body which knows how to triumph over illness and over the miseries of the sleeping world.

Close your eyes to the fleeting fires that sadly seduce you, and turn your gaze toward the Body of Fire that darts where there is no limit. If the secret Sulphur wins over the arsenical one it obtains the Stone, white as silver, shining and strong.

Keep this image constantly present: Saint Michael with a *spear* (solar sign) pierces the *Dragon* (matter) so that its blood (of life) can pour out.

Over the Primordial Waters (darkness) shot the dart, or spear, of Fire (will) and there emerged the *Light* from which all things are made.

55. If you are not mature, the serpent of time will clutch and seduce you; if you are not ready, uncertainty will offer you reasons to delay; if you do not love the Art, your thought will disperse and scatter in a thousand sparks; if you do not

dare, fear will hold you at a standstill. The "Pathway of Fire" is for those who have a single eye (unicorn).

56. Your mortal fire holds Immortality within itself. Immortality is a *certainty*, not a problematic possibility. What you require to win it back is, above all, Dignity, that Dignity which you lost in the mill-streams of time, confining yourself in a life of sleep and oblivion.

57. Immortality is not attained through the noise of speech, but through the voice of the Word. Sound is Fire that vibrates and darts dissolving, transforming, mortifying and exalting, reducing the fires to ashes and at the same time lighting the Fire that no water can quench.

58. Do not light the philosophical furnace if you are not cast in steel or do not know how to dominate and direct the flash of lightning that darts through the infernal darkness of incompleteness. This is and will again be repeated to you.

The "Pathway of Fire" imposes *Regal Dignity* and mercurial awareness. Fire must rise up and cut through every limitation in those who are worthy to approach the virginal beauty of the Goddess.

59. You must rectify, purify and exalt the Goddess-substance to Heaven. You must dominate, cadence and finally stop the chaotic movement of the Goddess.

Desire-passion constrains; self-assertion, vanity and pride are binding. You must tire out the "thirst" which demands profane water. You can dominate and transform the Goddess only if you possess solar (☉) *independent will* which draws incentive and life from its own existence and being. «Whoever collects and reabsorbs himself around the mercurial focal Pole does not reach out any more toward exterior and profane events».

60. The Goddess of ravishing beauty is shining Fire; she blinds the weak but makes the strong immortal.

One who does not dare with Dignity will lose himself in the uncertainty of his inferior stature.

61. Your "vessel" ($\ominus$) is condensed memory. Radiant and mercurial Fire slowly dissolves and frees the substance from its crystallizations, which implies making your "vessel" volatile and light. Your destiny is in the power of Fire and the "Pathway of Fire" points the way to manipulate it.

62. Your passionate body (irascible Soul) (ϕ) is an amalgam of humid fires that bind you to the object-event of passion-desire. This attractive-repulsive fire must be distilled and made neutral by you. You must split up the amalgam. You are left with a free, light and at the same time "fixed" mercurial "sensitivity" which, being able to contemplate, is not attracted by the gravitational power of metals and minerals nor by their root: the black Dragon covered with scales. In this state you may act, if you so wish, but as a true Architect.

63. Mind is a molding fire and part of the universal Fire; it can forge prisons and anguish but also the Beauty of Harmony; it can bring suffering or Bliss. Act like the Great Architect of the Universe. Imitate Nature.

64. To comprehend the infra-human or philosophical Fire means penetrating the mystery of the entire human compound as a projecting, molding and creating factor. To direct the

infra-human Fire means determining one's own destiny within the ambit of the laws of the cosmos.

65. If the spiritual Sulphur is comprehended and dominated it can shape favourable and wonderful events. If it is abandoned to itself, it cannot but cause irritating, strident conflict and incompleteness. Earth, water and air must be dominated, rectified and balanced. When, within the individual, earth, water, air and fire are in harmonious correspondence, the focal Beauty of the square shines and the construction of the Temple proceeds. When you have conquered the Antimony, the Venerable Old Man – father of all metals – you are dominating over substance.

66. The mercurial Center is the Demiurge and the solar Fire is the tool-mediator-*logos*.

The Demiurge, by means of its *Logos*, vibrates the Word of rectification, transfiguration and unification of the Fires.

67. First of all you must bring yourself to the *Center* of your focal system (☉), then – by dosing the Fire – you must unify the Fires, then direct the Fire and "separate" the Volatile from the fixed, the eagle from the lion. Then, if you dare, holding the *salamander* firmly in your hand, resolve mercurial Fire into Sulphur (🜍), into incorruptible and incombustible Fire.

68. For the construction of the Temple of Light you must pay attention to three things:

a) Proper tones relationship of tones.

b) Geometry of the lines of force.

c) Daring dignity.

The individual is a combination of seven main centers of Fire which, if comprehended, coordinated and integrated, can unite into the one Fire (*suṣumṇā*). Dominion over this Fire means holding one's own destiny in one's own hands. But remember, you must create the proper relationship between the Fires, a geometry of the lines of force such as to create perfect equilibrium and daring Dignity, otherwise the "poisonous serpent" may keep you in the vice of uncertainty and doubt.

The seven main centers of Fire (in the *Vedānta* Tradition they are called *cakras* – wheels of light-fire) are situated in the vital or prāṇic body and are the accumulators and the transmitters of energy; they are related to their corresponding glands in the endocrine system:

1. *Mūlādhāra* = the center of the coccyx
2. *Svādhiṣṭhāṇa* = the sacral-sexual center
3. *Maṇipura* = the sensory solar plexus
4. *Anāhata* = the center of the heart (the thymus gland)
5. *Viśuddha* = the center of the throat
6. *Ājñā* = the center between the eyebrows
7. *Sahasrāra* = the coronal center, which synthesizes the other six centers

69. A burning *thirst* spurs you along the alleys of conflict and mortality. Until you catch hold of the resolving shaft of lightning, no matter how much you may try to *assert* yourself, it is always the sublunary phantom that is in command; no matter how much you try to *plan*, it is always the chaos of the Dragon that enjoins you. Know this, however: one who dominates can be dominated, you must make the Volatile fixed

and immobile. This makes you complete; thus your Harmony will impose balance upon pure change.

If I speak to you of will, this does not mean that you must exert an effort or a tension as if faced with an obstacle; true will is free from strain, tension and nervous rigidity; it is something that springs from the world of non-resistance, outside of the time-space dimension; it is a free, innocent, subtle, dry act; it is the flight of a swallow darting upon the perfect stillness of its wings.

70. I mentioned above the seven *cakras*[1] or centers of force which are situated along the spinal column. Three of these are particularly important because they correspond with the three states of consciousness: $\ominus$, $\u263f$ and $\u2644$, or with the state of matter (gross body), soul and spirit.

These three *cakra* or centers of force are:

Mūlādhāra = $\ominus$ Earth – Individualized Fire – Lead

Anāhata = $\u263f$ Air – Radiant Fire – Mercury

Ājñā = $\u2644$ Ether – Incorruptible Fire assimilated to $\odot$ or Sulphur

The individualized material Fire operates by means of the *Maṇipura cakra* (the sensory solar plexus), *Svādhiṣṭhāṇa cakra* (the sacral center/sexual energy) and *Viśuddha cakra* (center of the mind), with the latter acting under the influence of the former two.

The radiant Fire operates by means of the *Anāhata cakra* (the center of the heart) and the *Viśuddha cakra*, this time the latter is acting under the influence of the *Anāhata cakra*.

---

[1] For an in depth knowledge about the *cakras* in traditional *Yoga*, see: Raphael, *Essence and Purpose of Yoga*, Element Books, Shaftesbury, Dorset, UK.

The spirit of the incorruptible Fire operates by means of the *Ājñā* center: the Eye of Śiva.

Before rectification, the *Anāhata cakra* directs its petals (it vital rays) downward to nourish the *Maṇipura* and *Svādhiṣṭhāṇa cakra*; after rectification it directs its petals upward to feed the *Viśuddha* and *Ājñā cakra*. Thus there is a distinction between the two Mercuries, one (☿) is under the lunar influence of psycho-physical individuality, the other (☿) under that of the Universal Person (♃). These correlations can help us to grasp the fact that there is a sole Initiatory Tradition with several different linguistic expressions.

71. Which ones are the fires holding the radiant mercurial Fire in the individualized expression?

Three powerful fires force the King and the Queen to sacrifice; they are:

1. the fire of desire-emotion-passion.

2. the fire of sexual creative energy.

3. the fire of self-assertion and self-expression in the form of the psycho-physical ego; this is the shadow created by the qualities of the Dragon.

"Mortification", or the "Black *Opus*" (*nigredo*), involves rectifying these fires and means *laying them bare* so that, once they are consumed, one may offer up to Heaven the substance which is thus distilled. The mental fire, under the influence of these individualized fires, acts for their gratification making the substance increasingly reactive toward and sensitive to that line of action and expression.

As a result, the substance, thus permeated and saturated, requires the same pattern of behavior to be repeated. Constant repetition of such behavior strengthens the individualized organ. The being is therefore determined by the power of the saturnine fires; this makes one realize that pure Mercury has fallen under the sway of lunar forces (☿).

When the mortification-rectification is completed, the consciential mercurial Fire is freed, and it can move from the three lower *cakra* up to the *Anāhata cakra* which represents the *Center* of the whole being, while the individualized center is represented by the *Maṇipura cakra*. One might say that the three lower *cakra* are those humans share with animals, while the three upper *cakra* are those shared with the Gods.

Therefore, we have to transform the three lower fires into the three corresponding upper Fires: the fire of egoistic desire into spiritual Will and ardor toward the High, which coincide with universal Law, Order and Harmony with the Principle; the sexual creative fire, dominated by the Dragon, into intellective and intelligent creative Fire, dominated by the *Logos*; the fire of self-assertion and selfish expression into Self-realization or Knowledge-Awareness of oneself as universal Principle or Sulphur.

Geber states that the Fire of the Philosophers contains within itself, «two causes of corruption and of impurity, the first is an inflammable substance, the other earthly dregs or impurities»[1].

72. All of this can be summarized in the following explanatory table. The rectified focal center of consciousness (Mercury of the Sage) operates by means of these *cakra*:

---

[1] Geber, *Summa Perfectionis Magisterii*, III, I, II.

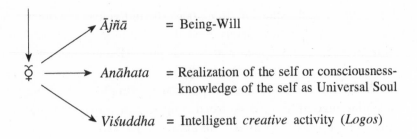

The non-rectified Center of consciousness (common or vulgar Mercury) operates through the following *cakra*[1]:

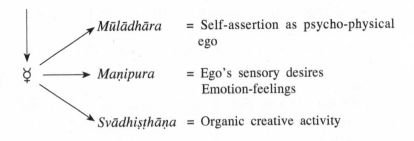

«The entire secret of Hermetic Philosophy consists in obtaining pure Mercury, that which was there before it was mixed with any other metal (that is before falling into individuality, specialization or particularization). This is the Mercury-Principle

---

[1] For a further view on the interrelationship between the *cakra* see also, Raphael, *The Science of Love*, 29-31. Aurea Vidyā, New York.

as distinct from the vulgar Mercury, which is as if dead when outside of the universal Mine, because its inner Fire is dormant and cannot act unless activated by the Mercury-Principle»[1].

«Mercury is called the Spirit of the Philosophers because only the Wise know the secret of turning it into spirit by freeing it from the prison of the body (of the individualizing process) in which nature had cast it»[2].

«And thus the convergence of the various symbols is made clear: to separate from the body means to make the life-principle (Water or Mercury) move into the non-individualized state; transition from "fixed" to "non-fixed" is therefore a "solution"; freeing what the body enclosed is "extraction"; returning to the original state is "conversion to the Prime Matter" and "making of the Mercury of the Wise". Finally there is "conjunction" when the two states are hypostatized and in the transformation one witnesses the effective rejoining of specialized life with immutable life, which, however, is not external to it, but lies as if stunned and dazed at its own very root»[3].

---

[1] A. J. Pernety: *Dictionnaire mytho-hermétique*. Paris 1758.

[2] *Triomphe Hermétique*, 141.

[3] J. Evola: *La Tradizione Ermetica*. Edizioni Mediterranee. Rome. – English publication, *The Hermetic Tradition*, Inner Traditions, Rochester, VT, U.S.A.

Separation (Albedo)

73. The rectification and stabilization of the mercurial Center are followed by the "Separation". The *Water,* or the Magnesia, has been purified and restored to its virginal condition. You have restored the "harlot" to its purity. The mercurial Center feels freer and lives almost in a state of imponderability, escaping the electro-magnetism of individualized Fire. This "neutral" condition grants it a position of supremacy and Dignity which it did not have when, trapped within the chaotic whirling of the restless Goddess, it had to submit to the law of "necessity".

Dignity means living and contemplating with the eye of equanimity and positive detachment; it also means not to marvel at anything because everything is in its proper place. Dignity belongs to one who, though living in this world, is not of this world. Dignity is not a concept but a *way of being*, it cannot be taught but must be grasped and incarnated by those who have the requirements and the qualifications. It is beyond all psychological dualism and good-evil itself.

74. If doubt strikes you, seize the lightning of Knowledge and of Art and rend the opaque veil which imprisons you. "Saṁsāric blackness" is resolved by the light of the Radiant Fire and the power of your Gold.

75. Let your Magnesia – now whitened and rectified – be a zither. Let harmonic sounds ring forth and enchant men and Gods. Space responds to the Beauty of Accord. Know that Alchemy is named by some Philosophers as the Art of Music. Our First Matter is portrayed as an Old Man wearing a crown and holding a zither in his hands. By means of sound the elements may be transformed from the *crude* to the *living* or philosophical state; they may be exalted or appeased. Orpheus is represented holding a lyre with which he *soothes* the *poisonous Serpent* that dwells within the wild beasts.

76. Fire takes delight in fire, Fire vanquishes fire and Fire resolves fire. Fire is its own mother-father; it is self-sufficient because it proceeds from itself and returns to itself.

Fire in its formal, manifest condition is bipolar. The being that seeks to resolve itself must unify the focal polarities, must quench the fleeting fires so as to find itself again within the quintessence of Fire.

77. Brandishing the lightning, fight the phantom of chaos that has trapped you within the swamps of mortality and of becoming.

From the region of change enter the region of Being, which is heavenly, non-combustible, homogeneous, invisible Fire, not subject to corporeal dimensions.

78. What really matters is to make yourself *positively active*. One moment of distraction and you find yourself in a passive, lunar and subjugated position.

You must oppose the dispersive, fleeting and dissipating fire with the concentrated, enlivening Fire which is collected and rotating around its own axis.

79. Sleep has veiled and weakened your radiant Fire, your Gold. You must awaken and recognise yourself in your splendor and in your immortality. The lunar world, however alluring, will lead you to oblivion and to the false emphasis of excitement.

Do not replace the flaming Sun with the weak reflection of the moon. Philaletes says (*Introitus*): «... at the outset it (☉) is dead; that is to say, its life-giving strength is hidden within the hardness of the body... but if it bathes in our Water, it is born again, regains vitality and becomes the Gold of the Philosophers»[1].

80. When the rectified mercurial focal Center rids itself of the earthly body of Fire, it enters its state of radiant Fire and expresses itself with a Joy that exalts all. When your water is purified through sublimation, it evaporates and you find yourself as Air (☿) in freedom.

81. Reach the dwelling of "Those who are" and no longer become – the Citadel of the Awakened, that place without boundaries. Only the power of Fire can transcend the dissipating fascination of fire.

82. If you love Immortality, seduce the virgin Goddess and transfigure her in the Embrace that shatters time.

83. The seed must die and split open to allow the birth of the Body of glory. Strike the seed of Liberation with lightning, kill the living and give yourself up to the Fire of

---

[1] I. Philaletes, *Introitus apertus ad occlusum Regis Palatium*, XIII.

the Art. The work must go on and the Body of mercurial Fire must fix itself to its Immortality.

84. When you have *identified* with the everlasting Fire, your human consciousness, dominated by the Furies, will be deprived of its support and your heaviness will be transformed into the *speed of light*. Only thus will you become free, win back your "remembrance", veiled by the phantasmagoria of phenomenal illusion and resume the Dignity that belongs to you.

85. If you have daring, follow with Dignity the phases of separation and the removal of supports.

If you have learnt to fly, your consciousness will not withdraw within the solid, but will take flight toward the peak of Liberty. This is the flight of the Dragon. During this phase the dominion of Fire is important, as you might fall: the very strength of Fire, thus liberated, might overwhelm you. This phase is laden with dangers.

86. If you have daring and Dignity you discover yourself to be All-pervading, mercurial Fire (☿), but you will no longer be that individualized, metallic ego with a name and a form. The lunar ego has disappeared, but so has its solitude and incompleteness.

87. Remember therefore: first of all you must establish yourself as the positive focal Center of your inner Temple. To lift the world you must prepare an adequate support-lever. Rectification and fixation will lead you to recover this Center. This is the first extraction of the Mercury from the Mine; with this operation you have turned your lead-body from positive to negative and your Gold from negative to positive. Then you

must *separate*. What binds you to the solid is the force-desire-thirst for individualized life. Solar Fire must distil the fluid or liquid Fire. By suspending your desire, thirst, and greed you lay the foundations of your true separation. Therefore you must sap the thirst that demands thirst, the greed that seeks greed and the humidity that operates within your philosophical Egg.

Condensed or terrestrial Fire has metallized and constrained both radiant Fire and sulphureous Fire. You must separate the Immortal from the mortal, the Real from the unreal so that, gradually, condensed Fire turns into "ashes". During this phase be careful, do not fall prey to fear because your consciousness would be brought back to *earth* and the doors closed. On the other hand you must learn to "die" while living; if you abandon yourself to passivity you will simply enter into a *trance*, but this is not in conformity with the "Pathway of Fire". The "Pathway of Fire" is solar, active and conscious. You will hear the "humming of bees" in a whirl while the consciousness withdraws.

88. You should learn this very important fact: "separation" can have two different destinations. The one you reach by the road leading to the lower subtle world, the other you reach by the road toward the upper subtle world.

There are some who, by means of psycho-physical practices, are able to separate themselves from their dense physical bodies and "hover" within the sphere of *feeling* rather than *will* and *knowledge*; that is, they are in the individualized psychic sphere. In this case, what has happened?

The psychic ego, characterized by the projecting sensorial mind, by feeling and by cellular instinct, has dissociated from the dense physical body ($\ominus$) and entered the hyper-physical sphere which Western Occultism calls "astral". But such a change of state (this is what normally happens to most individuals when they "die" to their physical bodies) does not modify either consciousness or the vision, nor the direction of the being; this state still remains within the ambit of the individualized psychic sphere (☿); it is a mere extension of individuality and it is not the rectified mercurial Center (☿) but, once again, just the psychic, lunar ego or vulgar Mercury. The blemishes that this vulgar Mercury may have had on the physical plane have been moved by the Mercury onto the lower subtle plane. If "alchemical separation" were this simple coming and going to and from the "world of the *Manes*" and the corporeal world, then Alchemy would be just a great illusion; one could say, a huge hoax. This transition is consciously carried out by trained *mediums*, by many persons who operate within the field of parapsychology and by some under the effect of certain drugs.

Even though from this level it may be possible, in certain cases, to intervene upon the gross corporeal dimension by means of the *ether* element or *ākāśa* – son of Saturn, or alchemical *antimonium* – this does not change the above consideration.

89. As long as one operates within the infra-individual (gross or subtle) sphere, alchemical, initiatory or Philosophical death has not taken place. What counts, in initiatory terms, is the "trans-formation" of the individualized psychic state (☿) into the universal spiritual state (☿), or of vulgar, lunar Mercury into philosophical, solar Mercury under the influence of the Sulphur-Spirit (🜍), or the winged lion.

In *Vedānta* terms, this means the trans-formation of the *ahaṁkāra*-manasic (strictly human condition) into *ātmā*-buddhic (divine condition).

The breaking of the psychic ego level must take place at this critical point in consciousness. This break implies passing from the mortal to the immortal, from the particular and individual to the universal and archetypal, from the unreal to the real, from the *pitṛyāna* pathway (the way of the ancestors) to the *devayāna* one (the way of the gods).

In qabbalistic terms one might say that the breaking of the psychic ego level occurs with the solution of the lower quaternary (*Nezach, Hod, Yesod, Malkuth*) and with the transfer of the mercurial Center into *Tiphereth*. This is the rectified Mercury (☿) extracted from the cave of Saturn, intermediary between the Celestial Jerusalem and the Terrestrial one (for more details of this qabbalistic *Opus*, see further on).

90. In *Vedānta*, the first pathway is called *pitṛyāna*; here separation represents only the detachment of the dense physical element from the vulgar Mercury, whereby one remains within the sphere of the individualized psyche, therefore returning to the plane of gross duality.

The second pathway is *devayāna*, the solar way of the Gods and immortality. Here it is not the dense physical element that, having reached full fruition, detaches itself from the vulgar Mercury; it is the rectified mercurial Fire that consciously and willingly frees itself from the ties and supports of the physical body, that of Saturn. The term *separation*, therefore, assumes its true meaning, that is, the *solution* of the individual psychic compound and the *fixation* of the solar Mercury (☿), beyond psycho-physical duality. This is true initiatory Death, the death of the Philosophers, but at the same time it means birth within the sphere of immortality. The "twice born" (*dvi-ja*) of the Hindu tradition represent those who are born again to Heavenly Life.

Once our substance has been rectified of impure crystallizations and of saline coagulations, the mercurial Center becomes radiant and turns toward the First Fire or the Sulphur of the Philosophers. The separation is then effected by the mercurial Fire-Center that leaves the lunar subtle level, which is the goal of the non-transfigured individual, and flies up toward the *ātmā-buddhi* sphere, toward *Tiphereth* or the Universal Sulphureous Principle (for further clarity see the diagram on page 58).

91. «What can I tell you, my son? I have only this to say to you: seeing within myself an immaterial vision, come true by divine grace, I emerged from myself to enter an immaterial body and now I am no longer the one I was before, but I have been generated in the intellect. This cannot be the object of Teaching and it is not the object of that material element we can see; for this reason I have no concern for the compound form that I possessed before. I no longer have color, nor touch, nor size: all these are alien to me. Now, my son, you see me with your eyes, but you cannot grasp what I am by looking at me with the eyes and the sight of the body; not with those eyes can you see me now, my son».

«What is true, then, oh Trismegistus?».

«That which is not disturbed, my son, which has no limits, which has no color, no form, which is not subject to change, that which is bare, luminous, comprehensible only to itself, the motionless good, the incorporeal»[1].

This Soul or Mercury of the Philosophers, made of Knowledge – according to the *Upaniṣads* – is as white as radiant silver (*Albedo*) and subtly penetrates all things. All productions at the level of the Sephirothic quaternary originate

---

[1] *Corpus Hermeticum*: XIII, 3-6.

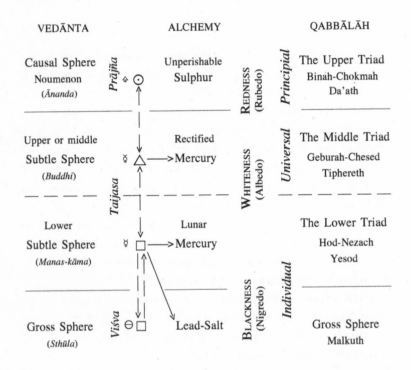

from this Body of light, of radiant Fire, and therefore every composite thing returns to it.

When the Substance-Goddess whitens, the King has vanquished death and conquered immortality; that is not the mere larva-like survival which follows the natural solution of the lead under the influence of Saturn.

In order to be, this body of Fire or of Glory does not require the support of Saturn; its reality can subsist in states and modes of existence that transcend the metallic and mineral condition; it is pure, essential Mercury, having the nature of Prime Matter, with the power to penetrate and pervade all metals and minerals.

92. Where does the transformation of lead into Silver or of black into white take place?

«The operation takes place in the heart, and here the gate of Heaven is struck with violence»[1].

«In the most secret chamber of the heart»[2] rests the philosophical Mercury unseen by profane eyes.

In carrying on the *Opus* it is vital to reach perfect equilibrium between the various purified and sublimated fires (rectification), equilibrium and neutrality as these allow the possession of the fixed and stabilized Volatile. Only by starting from it can the work give positive fruits, so it is well to insist upon this to avoid mistakes which may cost one even... the life of the "vessel".

Keeping all this in mind, one may proceed with the elevation of the earthly Fire (*Kuṇḍalinī*) so that the Virgin or Queen

---

[1] G. Gichtel, *Theosophia practica*: II, 5. Ch. II, *Introduction*: 5

[2] Dante, *Vita Nova*, II, 4

may join the Groom or King in the thalamus (nuptial bed) of
the heart (*Rebis*). From this point of view the separation may
be seen as a "conjunction". The physical Fire, denuded of its
passionate (flammable) and instinctive (watery) superimpositions,
may join the soul's mercurial Fire thus creating a single Fire
of such power and radiance as to make all things new.

There are different operative modes for elevating the earthly
Fire and joining it with the Celestial one; modes which should
be suited to each individual being, because each one is characterized by certain inclinations and qualifications and by a
certain position of consciousness. In fact, in the East there
are different kinds of *Yoga* (conjunction of *śakti* with *puruṣa*)
which respond to the different positions of consciousness of
each disciple.

93. If you follow the way of the *Qabbālāh*, I can give you
these suggestions to help you at the operative level.

Finding yourself in the Sephirothic quaternary (*Nezach,
Hod, Yesod, Malkuth*) and considering that the transcendent,
transpersonal point is in *Tiphereth*, what must you do? (see
the Sephirothic Tree on the opposite page).

Nezach is the Venus-Mother of individualization, the daughter
of *Binah*, the Great universal Mother, the principle of manifestation. As second cause of creation, all her impulse, power and
blind thirst is like an impetuous River which inexorably sweeps
everything that exists in the quaternary downward toward material objectification, (*Malkuth*). This blind force which pushes
downward, toward involution must be *channelled*, *cadenced*,
checked and *turned* upward in the direction of *Tiphereth*[1].

---

[1] For a deeper knowledge of the Qabbalistic Teaching see, Raphael, *Pathway of Fire*, Initiation to the Kabbalah, S. Weiser, York Beach, ME, USA.

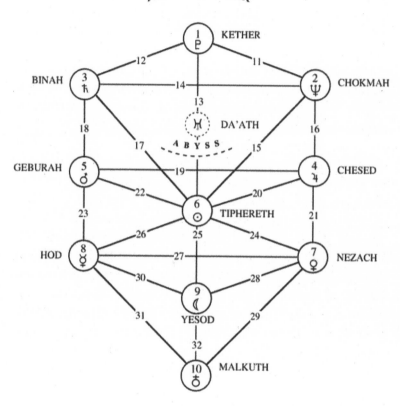

AIN SOPH AUR

Now your Gold, your Sulphur, is at the potential state, overpowered by this Sea which carries you adrift to *Malkuth*. You might well ask: is it in the nature of things that this should be so? No, not at all. This passive position of yours, this oblivion of yourself is unnatural. You may be lived by events, but you may also live and give direction to your life by having perfect dominion over your *Nezach* or over your *śakti*, if you wish to define it in *Vedānta* terms.

To obtain this result, first of all you must awaken your dormant sulphureous Fire; the watery Current awaits a Center, a solar Will, a direction-giving Intelligence, a concentrated, stable, fixed, positive and dominating Fire facing It. From this point of view you must close the doors of *Yesod-Malkuth* and, with the power of *Hod* reoriented, learn how to direct the Great feminine Current, giving it at first rhythm and then checking it. It is evident that at this point you are faced with two apparently different realities: Sulphur and Mercury, Sun and Moon, Man and Woman, King and Queen, etc. By the rule of the work you must realize an alchemical wedding between Sulphur and rectified Mercury, between the King and the Queen restored to her primeval virginity. The fruit of the wedding is a Son greater and more glorious than the Father-Mother: it is *Tiphereth*. What is the means that causes this union and fusion? Upon the wings of the power of Fire, the heat of Sulphur, of Eros-Love if you will, the celestial Wedding is realized. I shall tell you more: Eros is the Master of the *Opus*. And where will you find your Bride? Within yourself, because *Nezach* flows inside of you; in fact, up to now it has dragged and probably it is still dragging you impetuously down toward objectification in *Malkuth*.

What are your thirst for formal life, your desire for experience, the compulsion to acquire, those passions that push you into the current of non-being, making you impotent, dizzy and dazed? What is that dispersive power of your mind (*Hod*), that uninterrupted flow of imagination and projection, of thought and judgement that prevents you from finding concentration and single direction? What do you think it means *to lose yourself* in thinking to such an extent as to be lived, enslaved and alienated by it? All these things are the manifestations of *Nezach*, of Venus in descent, of earthly Venus. And this ceaseless, dispersive and alienating current awaits a Center, a conscious and steadfast Will.

Through the wedding, your Venus will turn Heavenly; sexual union at *Yesod-Malkuth* level is only a symbol of this sacred, truly resolving Union.

And what if the solar Center were unable to weather the storm of the potent and forceful Mother or Ocean, which produces and at the same time swallows up the fluctuating forms? The question is critical and very serious. If as yet you do not have that solar Dignity or that Will-Faith-Ardor which is able to impose itself upon the humid change, it is better to stop and postpone the *Opus*. The alchemical process demands the *composure* of sulphur as well as the power of Ardor, Daring and Being. Know that the Current of life which tends downward, is also full of "monsters", foul vapors and atavistic content-entities; it is the place where forms and events that no longer exist upon the plane of *Malkuth* are stored; it represents the unconscious and the subconscious of the entire individualized process, where you will certainly find everything and anything, and within this chaotic all, you could fall into alienation.

The reckless who approach this scaly and black quagmire, yet so full of great things, may be bent and broken to the extent of losing their individual identity, without having first conquered the Fire of Life. After the encounter with the Dragon one either emerges a victor or one is overpowered by its descending Current. Know also that once you have gone into this experience – and not simply in theory – you cannot turn back. The *solve et coagula* is a one-way journey; either you overcome the abyss or you are swallowed up within it. But if you have sufficient Dignity you will realize that the embrace with your Mother (alchemical incest) can lead you back to the awareness of your Immortality. As an encouragement I wish to remind you of this: «Therefore I tell you, whatever you ask for in prayer, believe that you have received it, and it will be yours»[1].

---

[1] *Mark*: XI, 24.

Unification (Rubedo)

94. It is appropriate to point out a few things: the alchemical *Opus* is a prodigious process of *solve et coagula*, of solution and integration, which operates at various existential levels. This *Opus* may consist in conquering – by means of solar Fire – the so-called vital body (*Yesod*), which is the expressive vehicle of the empirical and metallic ego, immediately above or just inside the dense physical body. This prāṇic-etheric body, "astral light", being silvery as the moon, is the quintessence of dense matter. By realizing this body, as many *Haṭhayogis* have done and still do, one obtains complete mastery of the four physical elements thus bringing the organic functions under control.

The *Opus* may also be a process of *solve et coagula* with regard to the prāṇic body and the *kāma*-manasic body (*Hod-Nezach*), the astral body proper or, in *Yoga* terms, the lower subtle body (*taijasa* = luminous, shining). This is another body, a mixture of the quaternary, through which the empirical ego expresses itself.

It may also be an *Opus* of *solve et coagula* concerning the *kāma-manas* body and the fixing of the Soul (*Tiphereth*). It is only at this level that takes place the breaking in the process of individualization and therefore in the ego-quaternary. This is the true "death" of the Philosophers, because one emerges from individualized becoming and achieves the universal or

Christly state. The Soul is the intermediary between pure Spirit (*Noûs*) and Matter (χώρα); it is the bridge that connects Heaven and Earth. The Christ-*Tiphereth* is the bridge that connects the kingdom of *Malkuth* with that of *Kether* – the Father in Heaven – the earthly Jerusalem with the Heavenly one. But the Christ-*Tiphereth* must still achieve what is stated in the Gospel: «I and the Father are one»[1], and *Kether*, we know, is the first determination of *Ain Soph* (the metaphysical One).

If the Brothers of the Art disregard this qabbalistic background or that of the Egyptian metaphysical Teaching, their *Opus* will merely consist in either separating themselves from the gross physical body (*Malkuth*) and operating on the sphere of the vital-prāṇic body, or separating even from this latter one and fixing themselves on the level of the astral body (the body of individualized desires and the field of illusions) – making that kind of "little astral journey" which is the topic of parapsychological literature – and therefore losing themselves in the world of *māyā*; or, finally, they might practice some kind of utilitarian chemistry (spagyric). Now, the goal of the Hermetic Tradition is not that of remaining confined in the world of *māyā* (vanity of vanities) but, on the contrary, that of wresting pure Being from the jaws of the *māyā* Dragon. If the practice is not sustained by theory, it may prove to be dangerous because it has no points of reference; and theory which is not followed by practice becomes sterile and inconclusive intellectualism.

The two Pillars of the Sephirothic Tree represent the Sun and the Moon, Sulphur and Mercury that must be resolved in the single Fire of the central column (the *suṣumṇā* of *Yoga*) which, in turn, leads to the metaphysical One. The two Pillars

---

[1] *John*: X, 30

have their base in *Malkuth* where the serpentine Fire lies in bondage.

The Alchemical *Opus* is a *solve et coagula method* which may be applied to a number of different existential levels. Thus, Alchemy proper is not a metaphysics, but an eminently practical method – just like *Yoga*. If it avails, as it *must*, of traditional Philosophy, it is simply as a background. Wherever this has not or does not occur, Alchemy gradually falls, as already mentioned, to the level of spagyric or the mere transformation of vulgar lead into vulgar gold; that is to say it becomes mere utilitarian chemistry.

95. While the first phase of the *Opus* consists in the rectification, the solution of vulgar Fire and the separation or conjunction of the two Fires (Lesser *Opus*), the second phase brings about a further *integration*, consisting of resolving the mercurial Fire ($\mathrm{\breve{\phi}}$) in the noumenal Fire or incorruptible Sulphur ($\mathrm{\Delta}$). Only then the three ($\ominus$, $\mathrm{\breve{\phi}}$, $\mathrm{\Delta}$) become a unity (*Tria prima*) and then Being expresses what *Vedānta* calls *sat-cit-ānanda*, or will-principle, universal knowledge-awareness and intelligent creativity; or, again, the Being may finally get to know itself in its fullness of expression (Greater *Opus*).

96. In a practical sense, the first phase is the more difficult of the two: it is not an easy task to extract the mercurial Fire from the cave of Saturn, to denude the substance by removing all kinds of encrustations ("terrestrial" and "combustible") or to fix the mercurial Center of consciousness ($\odot$) so that it stays without flickering, like a flame sheltered from the wind. «It is more difficult to extract Gold than to make it»[1]. Only

---

[1] *De Pharmaco Catholico*: XI, 8.

perseverance, self confidence, the rhythmical repetition of acts, etc., can lead to this goal. All this must be realized with the "proper dosage" of Fire.

«Comprehend everything according to nature and according to the regime; and do not seek anything else, believe me. And fire, I tell you, fire at the beginning, in the middle and at the end, doing nothing else, because Nature will move to accomplishment»[1].

«Make vaporing, digesting, continuous, non violent, subtle, enveloping, airy, close, non combustive, altering Fire»[2].

The various levels reached during the Lesser *Opus* are repeated – but at a higher winding of the spiral – during the Greater *Opus*. Sulphur and Mercury, the King and the Queen, buried within the philosophical sepulcher – exposed to the heat of the Fire – are extracted and united so that they become a sole thing (*Rebis*).

Thus a new *solve* is obtained to which a consequent *coagula* will impose itself.

This is the solution of the mercurial Fire and the fixation of the incorruptible Sulphur-Fire. Sun and Moon integrate *under the action of Fire*.

Mercury is simply the reflection of Sulphur, and Lead is merely the reflection of Mercury, and the three are but a unity that operates upon three different existential levels.

Spirit, Soul and Body (or, according to others, Soul, Spirit and Body, but it is really the same thing) are but a unity of consciousness which operates within the multiple states of Being. But it must also be said that what is generated is less than the generator, the effect less than the cause; the Spirit contains

---

[1] *Turba Philosophorum*, 22.

[2] Bernardo Trevisano, *De la Philosophie naturelle des Metaux*: 377.

within itself the Soul and the Body, and in its indivisible unity is complete in itself above and beyond time-space-cause.

97. If only a few are able to carry out the *Albedo* (whiteness) phase, "White *Opus*", very few indeed are able to arrive at the *Rubedo* phase, "Red *Opus*".
However, the road is open to the willing and to the daring.
Remember that if you travel the "Pathway of Fire" on each step of your ascent you have to follow the stages: focal Center (☉), rectification, separation or detachment, fixation and ascent. If you wish, after ascension you may descend into your earthly "chalice", consciously, willingly, freely, as a King or a Sovereign this time, because you have made yourself One and have reached the Dignity of Agni, the God of Fire.

98. To you, who aspire toward the true Rose + Cross (Hermetic *Rose* and Salt-*Cross* of the Wise), to you, true Son of Helios, I now dare give some indications to follow an *ars brevis*, a certain utterly dry road; it is the adamantine Way, the Pathway of the flash of Lightning, meant only for the very few and not free of danger.
With your consciousness withdrawn from the saline compound and from its molecular reactions, keep on retiring from the cloud of thought and mental images and from any ideation that vulgar Mercury may offer to you. When *silence* and stillness alone operate within you, then be *conscious* of a saturation of divine Omnipotence. You must not imagine; you must only be conscious of it; you must *feel* and *be* universal, immortal Fire-Power.
This incorruptible Fire has no ego or supports and does not belong to any individualized entity. It is this impersonal focal Center without circumference that is the Power, and not

you as psycho-physical ego. Feel yourself to be that impersonal Consciousness without circumference which rests upon itself and by itself. If, by any chance, a product of earthly amalgamation, a thought, an image, an emotion, an instinct and so on, should appear upon the screen of this Presence, "kill" this unwanted "second" with the all-powerful Eye of Śiva, or with a dash of saltpetre, *fixing yourself* more and more in the supreme fire of sulphureous Consciousness. If you have the strength, the power and the daring "to look" at this "second" while remaining *fixed* in yourself, motionless, unaffected, impassive – despite all, and above and beyond all – you will see the second (the vulgar fleeting fires) vanish, and the (Θ) calcinate.

By means of the application of a very high temperature (△), the "that which is not" vanishes before the "I am that which one is", the like mist in the wind: you must simply *affirm*, *reveal yourself* and *be*. If you are able, as the Eagle, to peck the dormant Lion, you will give it wings and immediately you must create identity with that.

Beware not to fall into this trap: it may happen that separation and unification with Sulphur prove to be an illusion because generally one has simply the *sensation* of being separated from the sublunary world; it is the mental or vulgar ego that *feels* detached from any possible thought and emotion; in other words, you may experience a reflection of true separation and unification through the sensorial mind which is a peripheral and indirect instrument of perception and knowledge of vulgar Mercury.

You may also achieve a certain degree of dominion over the energies, or *guṇa*, reaching an adequate level of freedom and independence of the ego; however, you may be liable to falling into complacency and abusing of this freedom remains. It is necessary to distinguish simple dominion over individualized, qualified energies, which obviously grants a relative freedom of choice, from authentic "alchemical separation" regarding the totality of the solar Center (☉).

At a certain point during "separation" the direction of the natural vital process comes to a stop; it would have continued its normal course if it were not interrupted by the alchemical experience. In this state the empirical or mercurial ego feels lost and frustrated because it lacks support, relation and expression; it smells the odour of death and fights to gain strength and vitality again. One needs steady awareness, intense Ardor for true Liberation and *love* of the Art to overcome this critical moment. Realization can be achieved by means of one last and daring leap toward union with the sulphureous Self. Remember that alchemical Ardor is an extremely potent tool, an *artifice* (from: *facere cum arte* = making or doing with art/skill), an appropriate instrument that acts to saturate your magnetic Aura which, in turn, *matures* events. Besides one can follow the deeply esoteric maxim of Saint Paul which states that «faith is the *substance* of hoped-for things»[1]. At this point of crisis, two roads may appear: one leading to the divine world and the other to the underworld. If there is adequate purification, or the will to be Self reigns, one will take the former pathway, otherwise the consciousness is knocked down and the *Opus* destroyed.

99. The *fixity* of which I spoke to you is not rigidity, because it has no psychic or physical characteristics; impassivity is not petrifaction and absence of being. Omnipotence is neither violence nor the urge to prevaricate, but it is a powerful

---

[1] Paul, *Letter to the Hebrews*: XI, 1.

calm, saturated by unshakeable faith-certainty. Keep in mind that there is a mass-force, a power of impact with respect to matter-substance; this power-strength is *quality* (*Vedānta* speaks of *guṇa*) which is consubstantial with matter and with bodies. When one talks of will, strength and power, the empirical ego conceptualizes these in terms of corresponding material qualities. The will-power of the Sulphur-Spirit must not be confused with the qualities of the *prakṛti*-substance, the Earth element.

True Power is Consciousness, Presence of *Being*, and Being is immortal, it is fullness, aseity and wholeness, as against becoming which is an attractive yet fleeting and enslaving phenomenon. Do not look at the world of phenomena or caress the sphere of compounds and masses, but with an act of Ardor, Daring and Faith-certainty, *fix yourself* in what you really are. For you, who are capable of daring, there is not even the need to waste time with the various phases of the *Opus* because, invested with an imperturbable Dignity, you have learnt to unleash that invincible Fire of Being before which there is no obstacle, whether great or small, capable of destroying the immortal and the supreme Awareness. For you who dare and know, even Mercury becomes the servant of Sulphur and is attracted and absorbed by it. For you who know, there is the certainty that – all told – Sulphur self-appoints itself as the sole and principial Agent. If others with the cold *light* of *Logos* or with the *heat* of *pathos*, gradually carry out the required alchemical transmutations, you leap into the timeless dimension, are aware of Being, and do not fall back from that state even in the face of the fiercest internal or external "enemy". From this metaphysical Height you may also be aware of the becoming in its metallic and mineral dominions, but for you it is only a chiaroscuro play, an appearance in which, joyfully or sadly, the mortals indulge.

This supreme, all-powerful Awareness, this sulphureous Self lies behind the gross vessel (⊖) and behind the volatile mercurial substance (☿), therefore it is behind the concupiscible and irascible soul, to say it with the words of the divine Plato. But I must remind you once again: it may happen that some *power* or group of powers, dissociates under the impetus of Sulphur which tends to detach and fix itself, and in this state of semi-freedom it may *bite* or *attack* you, plunging the solar Self into great difficulty. It would be very dangerous to let oneself to be overcome by the titanic forces of the lunar compound. The solar Self – enclosed in its *tomb*, as the divine Orpheus would say – must learn to find the sulphurèous Dignity which permits one, when confronted by these titanic forces, to resist and not desist from its Fixity and solar Will thus freed. If you are able to resist happily, these powers gradually return quietly to their "dens" (the bull led back to the den) and dissolve (the killing of the bull).

According to Orphism our Stone is the Soul interred and closed up in a *tomb*.[1] According to the Orphic ascent, this Volatile must be awakened, raised up to the Heavens and united with Dionysus. The Orphic *katàbasis* represents the Black *Opus* or *Nigredo*; alchemical rectification corresponds to typically Orphic purification. The separation of the Volatile from the Fixed corresponds to the detachment of the Dionysus within us from the titanic element, and the conjunction of Mercury-Sulphur corresponds to the union of the Soul with the Heavenly Dionysus seen as the universal spiritual Sun.

Thus, whatever occurs within your inner psycho-physical system (*athanor*) must not interest You, immortal omnipotent

---

[1] See also the Chapter "Orphic Ascesis" in, Raphael, *Orphism and the Initiatory Tradition*, Op. cit.

being. Let any "aggressiveness" on the part of your infernal world shatter to pieces in the face of impersonal, unflinching and invincible Impassivity; let all thoughts regarding the miseries of becoming crumble before the all-embracing Silence.

If you are able to fly directly toward the "I am that which one is" without any longer becoming; if you are able to *fix yourself* in this state of consciousness without hesitation, fear and conceptual or emotional discursiveness, then True Alchemy tells you that you have come back Home. You may at last recognize the fact that up to now you have been an authentic God in exile and not a simple "flame puffer".

Sulphureous Dignity

*«It is up to the Gods to come to me
and not to me to go to Them»*

Plotinus

100. In egotistical fragmentation there is no Dignity: in being overpowered by instinct, emotion, passion and ideation there is no Dignity; in reducing yourself to "mass consciousness" there is no Dignity; in being weak there is no Dignity; in being violent there is no Dignity; in being fanatical there is no Dignity; in credulity there is no Dignity; in despising others there is no Dignity; in physical and psychic dependence there is no Dignity; in hatred there is no Dignity; in fear there is no Dignity; in being full of restlessness and desire there is no Dignity. To live with Dignity one must have a precise inner orientation. It is not the words as such that penetrate and impress, but the fragrance of inner and sulphureous Dignity. It is necessary to awaken within oneself an invisible but penetrating quality capable of attracting the suprasensible Powers.

101. Dignity at the highest level is expressed by the state of Being. Therefore, be unity and reveal yourself as a single

dazzling "eye". Whoever is unity is a law unto himself and is beyond sensory polarity, beyond ego and non-ego.

102. If by Dignity you mean your professional and social respectability, you have not comprehended. The Dignity I am referring to has nothing to do with the beggar-ego. Dignity demands ascesis, detachment, immobility and silence.

Whoever has Dignity does not strive for acquisitions because he has within himself fullness and raison d'être.

The empirical, phenomenal, sensory ego prays and implores, the *true Entity* fixes its "gaze" and affirms.

103. There is no Power that can help you if you have no Dignity. The weak are bitten because they follow the law of their being-becoming, but do not think that you are being incited to overpower others.

Those who fear lack in Dignity. What should a *true Human Being* fear? Suffering? There is no suffering for one who knows the end right from the beginning; suffering cannot reach the incorruptible Fire. Death? There are words that do not belong to the vocabulary of the Immortal.

Life itself? Whoever operates with Dignity reveals himself as commensurable and does not allow himself to be lived. Living is for those who "come and go", but Being thrives on Being.

One may fall, but Dignity requires one to get up again composedly, with beauty, without noise, self-commiseration or regrets.

104. The "sleeping" beings live on phantoms and hallucinations which they take for real; they feed on opinions. The *true Entity*, being unity, is light unto itself. The "sleeping" beings, nourishing themselves on passions, are possessed by the scaly

Dragon: passion is the incarnation of a demonic, titanic power. To stimulate a passion in oneself, means summoning up the corresponding demon. But there are those who are capable of evoking with Dignity without being possessed. Anger, fear, violence and all other passions *give access* to the Dragon god of limitation and constraint.

Dignity requires one to *command* the demon and to *co-operate* with the Powers. That of *māyā*-becoming is a world made of laws, of manipulation of forces and of energy interplays.

105. One may be tricked, one may play, one may be above and beyond every possible game.

True Dignity belongs to those who are able to turn the wheel of becoming while at the same time remaining still in *metaphysical immobility.*

106. Dignity is a style of being upon the plane of multiplicity. To express this state is not a question of techniques, no matter how valid.

Dignity is the outcome of superior stature, therefore it is the effect of Realization. Whoever conquers Dignity may knock and the doors will open.

A good deed creates ties if there is attachment; the Entity of Dignity is one with Its own direction, and does not worry about the "second".

107. As long as the individual lives restrained by the form-image he has created in time, he cannot have metaphysical Dignity. The being must grasp the sense of its own Reality and not project an estranged image of itself. If you are an Eagle it is madness to believe yourself to be a creeping snake.

If you have Dignity, dare and assert, as the universal Fire, the green Dragon, the Great Agent or First Substance, or whatever else one may wish to call it, will be molded as a result.

108. Whoever has Dignity has no doubt, uncertainty, or anxiety about doing or not doing. Dignity requires one to be the incarnation of certainty. Knowledge is the instrument by which to grasp Dignity, which is not the fruit of fanaticism, hard-headedness, obstinacy, arrogance or ignorance. There is a *desire* to act and a *will* to be; the former is the fruit of the phenomenal ego that operates with effort, tension, and upon the plane of resistance; the Being affirms and proclaims with calmness, determination and certainty.

Whoever desires has no Dignity: the Entity of Dignity is "simplicity" which holds everything within itself. The complex obeys the simple, the mobile the immobile, the relative the absolute, the becoming the Being.

109. The Entity of Dignity does not theorize or discuss, digress or interpret and needs not convince: all of these belong to the saṁsāric ego which is in need of sympathy and consensus. The Entity of Dignity is immobile, it is the nocturnal Sun that shines at the zenith.

Dignity is Fire that knows how to burn and reduce to ashes, or it can light, ignite and mold. With Dignity, the ideation becomes expression, the word becomes realization and the gesture becomes command.

110. It is not a theory or an essay on Dignity that is given to you here, but the indications of a state; you can build your Temple with and on this Dignity.

Initiatory Teaching is not a matter of writing essays but involves precise tasks and authentic realizations. Therefore, remember: our Stone arises from the solution of two substances, the one metallic, the other mineral; the one dry and igneous, the other humid and cold. Now these two antagonistic substances, by means of the intelligent action of Fire directed by ☉, withdraw and decompose. From their death is born a Rose of the greatest splendor that has the virtue of unifying and harmonizing the four natural elements. When you have realized the Rose and the Cross the *Opus* will be complete and you will be a Rose + Cross; but then Dignity will certainly oblige you to live incognito; I might say, in the invisible.

II

ALL-PERVADING FIRE

Realization according to Love of Beauty

1. «But there is, though, a transcendent Beauty. In the sense-bound life we are no longer granted to know it, but the Soul, taking no help from the organs, sees and judges. To this vision we must rise and contemplate, leaving sense to its own low place».

«...and hence, with an identical method we have to search for both Beauty and Good... And Beauty, this Beauty which is also the Good, must be posed as the First: directly deriving from this First is the Spirit as Beauty; through the Spirit, the Soul is made beautiful. The beauty in things – actions and pursuits for instance – comes by operation of the shaping Soul which is also the author of the beauty found in the world of sense. For the Soul, a divine thing, a fragment as it were of Beauty, makes all things that it grasps and molds beautiful in the measure of their capacity».

«This, indeed, is the mood even of those who, having witnessed the manifestation of Gods or Supernals, can never again feel the old delight in the comeliness of material forms. What then are we to think of one who contemplates Beauty in itself and for itself, no accumulation of flesh and matter, no dweller on earth or in the heavens – so perfect its purity – far above all such things in that they are nonessential, composite, not primal but descending from Beauty?

Beholding this Being – the Choragus of all Beauty, the Self-Intent that ever gives forth and never takes – resting, rapt, in the vision and possession of so lofty loveliness, growing to Its likeness, what beauty can the Soul lack? For This, the supreme, absolute, and primal Beauty itself, fashions Its lovers to Beauty and makes them also worthy of love.

And for This, the sternest and the uttermost combat is set before the Souls; all our labour is for This, lest we be left without part in this noblest vision, which to attain is to be blessed in the blissful sight and which failing is to fail utterly. For not he that has failed the joy that is in color or in visible form, not he that has failed in power or in honours or in kingdom has failed, but only he that has failed of only This, for Whose winning he should renounce kingdoms and command over earth and ocean and sky, if only, spurning the world of sense from beneath his feet, and straining only to This, he may contemplate».

«But what must we do? How lies the path? How can we contemplate this prodigious Beauty, dwelling as if in consecrated precincts, apart from the common ways where all may see, even the non initiate?».

«To any vision must be brought an eye adapted to what is to be seen, and having some likeness to it. Never did eye see the sun unless it had first become sun-like, and never can the Soul have vision of the First Beauty unless itself be beautiful.

Therefore, first let each become godlike and each beautiful who cares to see God and Beauty»[1].

2. The individual is a resounding string that may be tuned to the note of the cosmic Musician or else may play disturbing and unpleasant notes. The most exalting Music is that which offers the beauty of Accord, and therefore noetic bliss.

---

[1] Plotinus, *Enneads*, I, 6: 4, 6, 7, 8, 9, translated by Stephen MacKenna. Op.cit. .(Minor revisions added).

There are arrhythmic souls and eurhythmic souls, each vibrating appropriate tonal proportions. Consonance-Accord with the universal is also called Love. Love is proper tonal relationships, it is appropriate chords of notes, and so it pours out the stupendous music of the spheres; Love is life-giving and transfiguring melody.

Two souls, or two vibrant strings that *meet* create a Love-Consonance, a Harmony, and such Beauty as to exalt the expectant space.

3. Two rays of color in accord create Consonance, two minds in consonance reveal radiant Love or all-pervading Fire.

Love-Harmony is Accord between two attitudes, two glances and two minds that exalt Creation.

4. When a negative pole opens its Heart to a positive pole, a flash of lightning bursts out and space enjoys the elation of Beauty.

5. To harmonize with the rhythm of the Heart is Love, to tune two strings to the vibrant Beauty of the Fire of Life means revealing flames of Love.

Love is Beauty that gives joy, free of any sense of possession and distinction.

Beauty is the effect of tonal chords, it is the right relationship of proportions, it is commensuration with the universal Truth. A rose radiates Beauty that leads to ecstasy; two Hearts capable of vibrating to rhythms of dance-like movement lead to ecstasy. Truth, Love and Beauty are syntheses of Life, the operative transfiguring "principles" for the empirical being who knows how to open up.

6. Melody is the outcome of two concordant points, while centripetal love is the effect of discordant notes.

There are thousands of books that teach many things, but only a radiant Heart is able to reveal the mystery of a budding flower or the fragrance and enchantment of a dawn.

7. My hands are the reflection of Yours,
   my face is the reverberation of Yours,
   my pupils are mirrored in Yours,
   my heart is a projection of Yours.
   I am in You and You live in me:
   we are One because You have no second.

8. The mind analyses, calculates and compares: the Heart synthesizes, comprehends and reveals.

Individuality builds barriers and offers reactions; the radiant Heart knows no physical, psychic nor spiritual circumferences.

9. In the great orchestra of creation there is nothing more seducing than an Encounter. When two Souls meet, angelic harmonics resonate all over space, creating consonance and eurhythmy.

10. Unveil the ecstasy of the Accord, forget the discordant subconsciousness. May the great gift of Love live within your Vision, tuned to the timbre of the imperishable Self.

Oh you who comprehend, through the lightning of the Fire of Love rend the darkness that oppresses you.

May your breathing be flight toward Beauty; savor the assonance of gentleness and inebriate yourself with the supreme Idea of Beauty.

11. Beauty is that which enchants, calms and elevates, because it corresponds to Truth; it is what leads to silence; it is full of Bliss.

Beauty is pure Comprehending devoid of "ego". Capture it with Dignity, in the silence of your Temple.

Beauty renders a sensitive living String joyful. It is unifying and all-embracing ecstasy and gentleness that makes you transcend all differentiation. Beauty exalts life that reveals itself. It unifies manifest beings. Beauty is a balanced Fire-Sound. Capture it and inebriate your expectant instrument.

12. There is a beauty and there is Beauty; the former is an emotional, image-forming desire of the sentimental, separate, conflicted ego: the latter is correspondence of parts, it is the grace of a gesture or, at a higher winding of the spiral, a vibration with Being: it is Life harmonized with Life.

13. Love is Beauty because Love is a dance that makes one *savor* (*rasa*) the union, the *taste* of Being, the intelligible Bliss; it is the sublime tonal Accord of principles;

Beauty is Love because Beauty is perfect commensuration with the Idea; it is the fragrance of joyful motion, the fulfilment of the Laws and the Order of the universe.

14. A star is a note, a planet is a note, a manifest entity is a note; when you have learnt how to harmonize them all, when you know, thanks to the Fire of Eros, how to create accord with them, you will be on the Way to Harmony, on the "Pathway of Fire", on the Way of Truth, on the Way of Beauty.

15. Resonate with the harmonies of the rainbow and enchant the ears of those who are distracted from the Music of the spheres.

Bewildered beings bend under the hammer of conflict. Instil the radiant Fire of Love-Harmony-Truth into the anguished eyes of men.

Turn those who knock into harps so that they may enchant the waters of space.

16. When the twelve harmonics of the Heart vibrate in the cosmic Space, life will reveal the splendor of Truth, Love and Beauty. Only then will the Music of the spheres be heard in all its seducing Harmony.

17. The "Pathway of Fire" is the Art of discovering oneself as universal Music. It is the Art of rediscovering oneself, knowing oneself again, thinking and acting in terms of Truth, Love and Beauty.

You are a Note that the great universal Musician has been playing since time immemorial. Discover yourself and reveal yourself as a vibrant Note; Life will respond to your symphony.

Remember that true music (*saṁgīta*) is able to shatter the cycle of birth and death (*vimuktida* = donor of liberation). In fact, the entire structure of the universe is based upon Sound.

If you discover your fundamental Note and you tune it to the breath of Eros, the body will respond to you.

Meditate upon the laws underlying the relationship between mind and sound, between consciousness and light or fire.

The physical body, insofar as it is organized life, is the result of sound and when it stops death intervenes; that is to say that the atoms and molecules break up and separate, because the *cohesive power* has failed.

18. Think of Accord, speak about partaking, give comprehension, move with the rhythm of Beauty, live the tone of

Love-Truth: the disciple of the "Pathway of Fire" proceeds with Dignity, with Composure, with Gentleness.

19. He who does not produce Accord remains alone with himself as "empirical ego". Solitude belongs to the living note that has not yet been able to find its place in the great orchestra of Life.

Often a note vibrates in such an arrhythmic manner that it finds it very difficult to harmonize with the great Musician.

If you wish to vanquish oppressive solitude, you must transcend individualized egoistical sounds and harmonize yourself with the thousand suns affixed to the canvas of the Great Architect.

20. When a heart opens up, *space* responds by natural law; if this does not occur it means that the note is the wrong one: Love-Harmony, like light, possesses particular vibratory frequencies.

21. Do not think that Love is what is expressed at the sensorial or instinctive level; these vibrations – especially when left to their own devices – are obtuse and discordant. They have never granted satisfaction to anyone, otherwise the human race would have been happy for a long time already. Often desire, and its consequent relief, is mistaken for Love which is neither desire nor gratification.

In desire there is appropriation, possession, bewilderment and one-sidedness; in desire there is spirit of preservation; in desire lie the seeds of conflict and of suffering.

All desire stems from a *restlessness* which urges one toward satisfaction and relief from tension.

Restlessness stems from a psycho-physical vibratory disharmony.

Disharmony, restlessness, desire and acquisition represent the hermetic Dragon that bites its own tail. Love does not germinate upon this soil; in fact, it can arise only when that soil has been cleansed, purified, rectified and sublimated.

Love-Accord is the mortification of the conflicting and separating "ego"; it is quiet and serene happiness, it is *pax profunda*. Love does not crave, nor does it yearn, compare, or judge.

Can Love desire Love if it is Love itself?

Can Knowledge want Knowledge if it is Knowledge itself?

Love is creative and transfigures all it touches; sensorial desire imprisons and blunts.

Love reveals sounds and pauses, swirls of colors and neutral space, and that is completeness.

In Love two Souls vibrate in freedom; in sensorial desire there is imprisoning gratification of psycho-physical needs.

Sensorial love is nostalgia for the lost Paradise. You do not need to acquire Love, you must simply reveal it: It is in you.

The proper evocation will call upon the radiant Energy which will, in turn, shape human life into modulated encounters.

22. Egoism is love of oneself, but it is often mistaken for true Love. In true Love there are tolerance, comprehending and *freedom*; there is forgiveness, absence of judgement and emotional silence; there is intelligence and *warmth* that bring about growth without compulsion.

Only one who has vanquished individualized Fire can Love.

23. Love is the unifying way par excellence. It implies giving oneself without conditions, without resistance, without the

interference of subconscious arrhythmy. To love, one must die to the separating ego, one must be necessarily and totally available.

In true Love every kind of desire is dead, every sign of egoistical life is gone and every individualized request is transcended.

There is nothing more precious than giving oneself, forgetting oneself and abandoning oneself to the elation of Union. The Principle is the crowning of true Love.

24. Restlessness, or disharmony, leads to desire and to the modification of consciousness. This in turn leads to imprisoning action and imprisoning action leads to continuous change and to the alteration of the vibrating String. Change and alteration of the String lead to time-space, and this to limitation and conflict. Whoever lives in conflict is discordant music.

25. Whoever rotates around his own Axis, whoever lives a Centrality of his own does not produce desire but simply reveals the Sound of the great Musician.

Whoever comes to the Center conquers all his own acoustic space and this is completeness.

Desire, or translatory motion or modification of thought, urges the individual toward acquisition, toward becoming and time-space. Whoever Loves has no need to modify his own consciousness because he has touched the entire circumference.

Whoever Loves does not need to alter his vibrating String because this resonates the perfect Harmony of the spheres.

26. Can there be enslaving action for a Self that is free of separateness and of appropriation?

To live by revealing one's own nature, or the nature of Accord, means to activate the space of Love. What can one possibly want, desire, accept or take if one no longer has that unachieved "ego" which is used to take, grasp, desire and accept?

You have to comprehend the Motion that needs no motion, the Action that needs no action, the Love that needs no love, the Fire that needs no fire.

When you express yourself as Action free of attraction-repulsion, your "sense of ego" will dissolve and you will be able to reveal pure Action, pure Motion, pure Being, pure Love, pure Fire.

Whoever is free of the "sense of ego" is without the attributes of the "ego" and whoever is without the attributes of the "ego" does not desire or compare, criticize or accumulate, seek or deprive, but simply reveals himself as Love-Accord of life.

27. To love others means to *reintegrate them* into our vibrating String. Thus, Love-Harmony is not an act of identification with the emotions of others and with body-forms which are the vessels by which Harmony has to reveal itself. It does not mean getting involved in or being carried away by the psychical movement of others; in other words, it is not passive weakness, but something more: it is resting in principial Identity, in the universal Note.

It is not to the condensed or individualized Fire that one must look at but to the very Essence of Fire.

28. Love is not weariness, passiveness or condescension; it is not pity, commiseration or indulgence; it is not a question of giving to others all they inconsiderately wish, demand or expect.

Love is Comprehension and where there is Comprehension there are also Vision and discernment, correct evaluation and knowledge of the event.

29. Heat is due to the acceleration of atoms and cold is due to their slowing down. Therefore the greater the movement the greater the heat and the greater the inertia the greater the cold.

Love reaches such a vibratory intensity as to create a furnace of Fire capable of breaking the chains of separateness. «God is a Fire that consumes»[1].

30. If you are in Harmony with the universal you comprehend its unlimited tonal qualities which it seeks to express through vessels-bodies.

It may be that in your present state there are expressions of life that displease you, but remember that these too are part of that universal Accord you long to realize.

To *comprehend* means to assimilate, accept, synthesize, unify and integrate.

31. Peace of Heart arrives when you have brought together again all the manifest polarities within it; when, having reached the unifying Accord, you are able to remain firm in your "Divine detachment".

Remember that as long as you operate along a certain *vital polarity* you may oppose other polarities. This means that you do not live, and are not in Accord with, the universal symphony. The Harmonic Being performs actions only to balance the "individualized forces", but is not attached to a particular energetic expression or to an action or to its fruit.

---

[1] Paul, *Letter to the Hebrews*: XII, 29.

32. The Harmonic Being, having offered up its "sense of ego" to the glory and to the Beauty of Totality, is in Love-Accord with the manifold living Notes.

There is no higher aspiration, no event more beautiful than *donating oneself* to the universal, than *offering oneself* to the noumenal Fire and *conceding oneself* to the all-pervading Beauty.

Whoever expresses Accord is attuned, upon the manifest plane, with the clod of earth, with the ripple of water, with the song of birds, with the flash of lightning.

33. The stars that pierce the vault of space indicate the route of cosmic Motion, in the same way as the all-pervading splendor of Fire reveals the source of every pulse of life.

34. If the One is a Heart that beats and gives rhythm to the flow of life, how can one think of existence except in terms of Heart?

35. If you begin to experience the all-pervading Fire, the Accord-Truth-Love, you will realize that it results in a silent and measured comprehension, it results in finding oneself in stillness at the consciential Center, it results in a donation of yourself that is not the outcome of submission.

36. If you live in the doubt of action you cannot reveal radiant Love or Harmony that exalts all things; Love-Harmony is being perfectly commensurate with *certainty*, with the immortality of all-pervading Sound.

From Love springs true comprehension of musicality.

Those who live in uncertainty are experiencing a sensorial movement of the ego, a state of non-knowledge and non-comprehension.

37. Two musical notes can be in tune because they belong to the same sound-principle.

Thus two *vital* notes can be in tune and can love and penetrate one another because they belong to the same Life-Principle.

Harmony and Love imply Unity because they contain in themselves the odds-evens, the negative-positive, therefore they are not the effect of an attractive-repulsive sensorial response, but represent an *encounter* with Life and with the vital principial Sound.

38. Do not be saddened by your detachment from the sensorial world; when you find a mode of expression absurd, you must be able to dare to fly toward a new World of Beauty where the certainty of immortality is expressed.

39. Rejoice in the ardent spirit, live the compassion of the Awakened, play the creative rhythm of the perfect Musician, heal the bleeding heart, listen to the song of the lark and the gentle murmuring of the stream.

Life overflows with radiant "quanta" and Being manifests the Beauty of its progress. Strengthen and donate yourself; within the universal whirlwind of life you are but a note.

40. It is not by running away from the world that you can overcome the world and it is not by running away from your passions that you can overcome the spectre of your passions. It is not by running away from pain that you can overcome pain and it is not by running away from your responsibilities that you can overcome events. Your victory over the sensorial world can be achieved through an intelligent psychological attitude, a conscious and heroic leap, and shattering of the

obstacle at the right moment. All-including Accord alone leads to transcendence, not flight, egoistical gratification or the projection of alibis.

41. Incompleteness can be overcome by the comprehension of and the ardor for the High, not by simple inhibition of thought or of action. A discordant instrument must be attuned on the basis of a fundamental note. And you, vital instrument, to which note are you trying to tune in?

The Authentic Silent One (*muni*) is a Sage attuned to the Principle, because he is Unity.

Know that if you adopt silence, and you are not a Sage, you are living on inhibitions. The Sage, having grasped the very essence of sound, becomes Silent. His Silence is not self-imposed, but is the natural consequence of having *comprehended*, of having quenched the fleeting fires and having resolved discordant, arrhythmic and strident sounds.

42. The construction of the Temple of Light must take place by comprehending and dominating the discordant notes so that they may vibrate in consonance with the Principle. At this point the human Temple becomes the vessel for the resonance of the harmonic and creative Sound produced by the great Musician.

43. What is an Accord with Life? It is an "attunement" with the rhythm of the universal Musician. But Accord requires the resolution of mortifying, discordant notes.

If you live in universal Accord you will find the solution to all your problems including those that concern the nourishment of your body.

44. To experience Accord means to *find oneself* in the oneness of Life, in the world of Ideas, in Being; it means recognizing all the various vital notes as expressions of the great universal Symphony.

Whoever is "attuned" becomes harmonic *unity*, a being capable of generating Gentleness and Beauty. Those who are attuned mold the sensible world to the notes of the intelligible world.

45. If you find it difficult to attune with Life it is because your individualized sounds are powerfully discordant. Sometimes it takes a long time to harmonize with the great Musician because one must adjust tones, octaves, wave-lengths, etc. Therefore, the Accord requires a *musical ear,* inner taste and a sensitive consciousness string, besides, obviously, the conscious and intense will to play.

46. Remember that there are souls that drown in Harmony and others that can master and direct Harmony.

The former are slaves to Beauty, the latter not only direct It but they can even transcend It and abide in the sphere of metaphysical Silence or non-manifest Sound.

47. Every form is a combination of notes, rhythms and harmonics; to disclose its archetypal composition means being able to create forms on the fundamental Note of the universal Musician.

A body-form has acoustic height, intensity and timbre of its own; it is the expression of a musical Order. Orpheus, used to eliminate all discord and arrhythmy from the inferior nature of beings with his lyre.

48. A lovely face is composed of a proportioned sequence of notes producing a luminous rhythm that may offer gentleness and sweetness to many entities.

If the soul that lies behind that face is also attuned to the archetypal sound of Beauty then the entire tonal context makes up a Harmony of such intensity as to capture men and Gods.

49. Ugliness and foulness are discordant notes which move away from the archetypal cadence of Beauty.

If the mental keyboard was not able to intone the hymn of gentleness and of Accord, this does not mean that the individual musician may not try again. Failure does not preclude success. What is needed is a training in musical sensitivity and, initially, detachment from the chaotic and neurotic sound of the sensorial world.

50. Accord gives Bliss which is not sensorial or acquisitive happiness.

The Accord we are speaking of here is of a supra-sensible order just like the Music that restores and delights.

The music of the sensorial world is the lower and distorted octave of supra-sensible music. How can the enchantment and the gentleness of dawn be contained in a sound, in a concept? How can that knowledge of cosmic melodic rhythms be rendered in "material" notes? How can the flow of the sound of universal Life be crystallized?

51. To open oneself up to the harmonics of the archetypal Sound is the task of the aspirant musician. To be on the pathway without learning the Art of *listening* and of *vibrating* means sure failure in the work.

Many aspirants want Accord-Harmony without re-educating their consciousness String.

52. After all, it is not the noise of the world incommensurate with Beauty, that prevents you from finding the right note and from vibrating Harmony. It is your consciousness, alas, submerged by such noise, that is unable to tear itself away from it and establish itself in an equidistant Point-Center.

The establishment of an "still center" within your sound space is an event that cannot be done without if you wish to pursue accord.

In all probability your "ego" is interposing a thousand obstacles of a sentimental, moral, intellectual nature and of other kinds; but, if you have decided, saturate yourself with the power of Eros and burn up the phantoms that confuse you.

53. In your subconsciousness dwell many irreconcilable notes that keep you in dissonance. But why do you turn to look at what is dead? Why do you bother with the dead?

«Let the dead bury their dead»[1] and turn, oh Magnificent one, toward the Beauty of the present that seeks revelation.

If you resist the tinkling of the discordant harpsichord rooted in the mill-stone of time you can overcome discrepancy and then it will be easy for you to attune yourself to the crystalline note of the great Musician.

54. The primordial Sound of life breaks up into many harmonics which, in turn, reverberate upon the keyboard of time.

In the manifest universe the many are interrelated by means of "umbilical cords " so as to create a synthesis of

---

[1] *Matthew*: VIII, 22.

life, a cosmic Melody. Accord, Truth and Love create the Bliss of living and the Beauty of unity.

55. Know that you are recognized according to the frequency of your vibration and therefore, according to the sonorous pitch and texture of the Fire-Light, the purity of the tone and the clarity of the timbre.

56. There is a Sound that absorbs and enraptures, which inebriates the translucent strings of the Heart-intellect and raises one to peaks of all-pervading Fire-Harmony.

The "Pathway of Fire" reintegrates one within the sphere of Beauty so that one discovers oneself as radiating Beauty. There are beautiful Souls that, like the dawn, are able to awaken to the exalting enchantment of this Truth.

57. Let the rose-bud of your heart bloom: its petals of fire will give you the Beauty of the Encounter. Radiant Love is the happy Meeting between what the analytical and separating mind calls opposites.

"Black" and "white" are reconciled in this unifying Encounter which is Love-Harmony-Truth. For those who express this Beauty-Reality, every dichotomy is resolved and life reveals itself for what it really is, not for what we would like it to be.

58. Turn what is unsightly into Beauty. In quiet meditation release flames of Love, because radiant Love is Harmony of thing-events that soothe weeping eyes which are petrified by the blinding disharmony.

But do not expect, oh you who seek to modulate your harp, that others will tune in with you.

Souls must be free to vibrate as they wish, because each kind of music is suited to the expression of that consciousness.

If you have comprehended the Art, then you must do nothing but play your stupendous melody because, among other things, it will shape the collective subconscious, bringing drops of balm to bleeding hearts.

Love that *silence* which radiates "quanta" of resolving fire and let yourself go gently and freely in the ether-alcove where dreaming and discordant beings oppress each other.

59. The things you must keep in mind are:

a) the empirical being's consciousness string.

b) the "inner hearing" of the noetic being.

c) the instrument of resonance upon the plane of expression.

The consciousness string in its present state must be made silent because it is used to playing individualized and discordant notes. Its music is not Accord, compelled as it is by offending vibrations.

The empirical or individualized being expresses itself through these egoistical vibrations which are not attuned to the Principle.

The "incarnate" vibrating string is of extreme importance: it must be rectified, modulated, attuned to the archetypes of Being. It is only a harmonic or a sonorous reflection of the noetic entity, but believes itself to be totality, unity and the fundamental note.

If you are responsive to the noetic being, by means of the mental instrument you can play eurhythmic music; if on the other hand you wander from it, you express dissonant, discordant and conflicting music.

Here is a graphic summary:

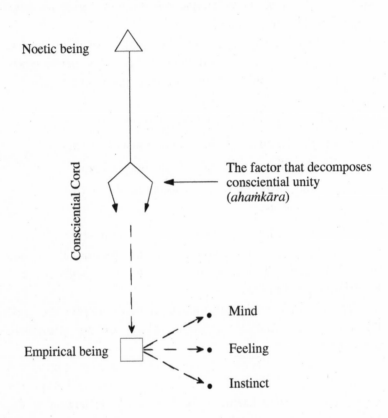

60. By what means can you perceive the tonal archetypes of Being?

With your "inner hearing".

You must therefore develop your inner hearing because it may be quiescent and latent; it is capable of being sensitive and of "appreciating" the qualities of Harmony. This kind of "hearing" belongs to an order that is above and beyond the sensory, but it can express itself also in a sensorial form. When it is developed, or actualized, it represents the modulator of rhythm. This immediate sensitivity for the appreciation of Harmony – innate to the noetic being and not to the rational or empirical one – confers the power to perceive the cosmic sonorous prism which represents the Whole.

Thus, in order to participate in a symphony or in a musical composition, you must possess a type of "musical ear" capable of perceiving and appreciating not only the single sonorous and orchestral elements such as pitch, volume and timbre, but also the harmony that represents the full-sounding and harmonic unity, the result of the accord and the cadences.

If you lack this inner faculty then you cannot follow the Pathway of Accord and Harmony. This is, therefore, a nec-essary prerequisite. You cannot become a Musician if there is no musical sensitivity in you; just as you cannot become a Philosopher if you are not "attuned" to the world of Ideas. In the East they speak of *rasa* which represents the "taste" or sensitivity that enables you to appreciate and evaluate.

61. The mental instrument is the "keyboard" with which you can play your music and develop your Harmony and Beauty.

This instrument must be controlled and re-educated; thus a harp must not only be tuned but the musician has to master it.

Our mental instrument is an out-of-tune and disorderly harp, therefore it plays chaotic, out-of-tune, frustrating notes.

Your physical body must become a vessel of resonance capable of giving timbre to your modulation.

If you are able to have:

- a pliant consciousness string capable of responding to the great Accord,

- an "internal hearing organ" sensitive to the Harmony of the Universe (*rasa*),

- a re-educated and willing mental instrument capable of shaping sounds,

- an efficient vessel of resonance capable of producing particular timbres,

then you can surely be initiated to the Music of the spheres, to the gentleness of Harmony and Love, to the law of Accord, to the perception of Beauty. Remember that the true Art is the expression permeated by the essence of divine Beauty.

62. An event is a form and a form is the result of mental vibrations. The mind is substance that vibrates. Remember: vibrating powers produce *precipitations*, they are activated by the unwavering attention of the *eye* fixed on the image. The microcosmic player with his keyboard can produce events-forms of marvelous beauty or of asymmetrical foulness.

Thus, alas, beings create ugly events because they have not learnt to use their mental keyboard.

The being who knows the Art creates commensurate and well proportioned notes, symphonies capable of enrapturing and giving completeness.

63. Your mind molds the tones and therefore the Accord.

The music of Life gives itself to those who love the Art. Your mind vibrates with either Beauty or unsightliness, and may resonate lower or upper octaves.

You must prepare your mental instrument first, then you can play it so that space may respond accordingly. While you are fine-tuning your instrument and your ability to modulate you need deep silence, utmost attention and concentration. Should the unmoving *center* that channels your mental energy be failing, the mental energy may very well dominate and overwhelm you.

Know that the external world is the world of effects, the internal world is that of causes. The sphere of the Self is the world of Being which makes causes and effects *appear*.

The external world is simply the reflection of the internal one: what *appears* on the outside is nothing but your real inner experience. All the circumstances and the experiences of life are merely the effects of your habitual and predominant mental vibration. Every mental vibration produces two effects: one which is radiant (quality), the other formal (number); quality in this case is expressed by means of a form-body of manifestation. The color of the form-body is determined by the nature of the vibration, while the color of the vibration is caused by the quality. Mental light-sound follows the laws of sympathy, tuning and affinity. Be aware of the fact that the laws of thought are the laws of *creation* and of active and objective precipitation. By being able to modulate your mental harp you can create universes of marvelous Beauty.

64. A material sound, like a mental sound, must evoke your inner Harmony.

Profane or sensorial harmony is a means for the gratification of emotions and instincts.

Sacred Harmony does not satisfy the emotions – although this may also occur – but it *exalts* your incarnated vibrating string and attunes it with the Note of Being and with universal hyper-tones.

Two individualities that meet exalt their instinctual, emotional and passionate notes; two Souls that meet exalt Accord with Life; they represent two resonating instruments within the great Orchestra of Creation capable of rendering Beautiful all that they touch.

Therefore, from individualized accord pass on to universal Harmony and from there rise up to identity with the fundamental note of the great Musician. Until you achieve this *ascension* of tones you will nonetheless be an apprentice musician.

65. The Music of which I speak is not that created by sensorial individualities, but that created by the Gods. However, the music of men that descends from *above* can be a powerful stimulation and can evoke the Harmony of the spheres in you. This is its function, or at least it should be.

If a musical piece – or a picture – does not elevate you and does not transfigure you then it is not music that corresponds to Accord. Abandon it as it is not for you. In the world of men there is music and Music.

66. A chord of two or three notes, being composed of different tonal values, forms a completely new *whole*. This happens because every single tonal value has its own peculiar vibration corresponding not only to a value but also to a number.

Thus when various beings are attuned to the rhythm of the universal sonorous Archetypes they represent a completely new *whole*, incarnating Harmony.

67. Manifestation is a complex of vibrations at different frequencies; the reciprocal relation of these frequencies determines an *event* which affects the entire creation.

Sound creates form; with *vibrations* you can "model" the atomic substance into molecules and structured forms. A range of vibrations causes a liquid to take on a specific configuration.

A world – like a formal human being – is born under the impulse of a Sound-Word.

68. When a musical string is plucked at its very center two things happen:

a) its vibrations double in frequency,

b) its sound is raised by an octave.

The noetic being is situated halfway along a string-consciousness the apex of which lies in the plane of Being and the lower part in the individualized empirical being.

If you manage to polarize yourself halfway along the string, your inner ear will open up because the string-consciousness is exalted by an adequate vibratory power or frequency.

Here is a visual representation:

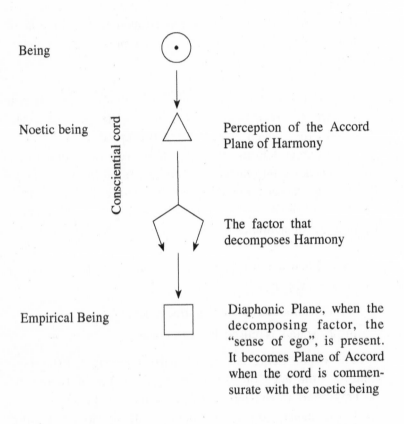

Being

Noetic being   Consciential cord   Perception of the Accord Plane of Harmony

The factor that decomposes Harmony

Empirical Being   Diaphonic Plane, when the decomposing factor, the "sense of ego", is present. It becomes Plane of Accord when the cord is commensurate with the noetic being

69. If the length of a musical string is shortened the frequency of its vibrations increases. Therefore if you consider yourself a consciousness string that, starting from the empirical being, stretches only up to the noetic being, then, by touching this string at its half-point you will obtain a strengthening of the emotion-mind; while if you have transcended the segment of individualized consciousness and you polarize yourself halfway on the string (that is in the noetic Being) you will achieve identity with the principial Sound".

70. What makes the empirical being arrhythmic is the "sense of ego" which is a prism that breaks up or decomposes the universal Sound, the Accord or symphonic Unity, thus giving rise to an isolated weak, low and opposing vibration and producing a sound that brings loneliness and conflict.

A harmonic, an overtone, is simply an element of the fundamental note, but if it believes itself to be the fundamental note, thus changing the nature of its sound composition, it falls into illusion-ignorance.

71. You are a "Harmonic" (quality-number) in the great universal Tonality of Being; comprehend the tonal laws, the harmonic relationships; discover the dominant Note; take up your place as a Musician and fill yourself with Harmony.

72. If you need a material support, take a musical instrument, play it with the *heart* and harmonize your mind to that sound until you become sound yourself; then capture the upper supra-sensible octave and abandon the support.

Harmony can bring about the "breaking of the ego level" so that you may find yourself to be "Music of the spheres".

Oh, what sublime sweetness!

73. If you are lucky enough to harmonize with an elder Brother already *attuned*, stay close to him and, having calmed your restless soul, "listen" to his rhythm and to his Harmony.

In this case too, one must learn the Art and be sensitive to the musicality of the eurhythmic soul.

74. It is a question of "inner ear", of stopping thought and, in the silence of the mind, listening to harmonic vibrations by simple induction.

If your psyche is still, if your consciousness is *open* – free of superimpositions – the miracle of induction will take place.

75. If the Beauty of the Accord you receive exalts you utterly, remain still because the merest wandering thought form may tear you away from the enchantment.

76. Give me your eyes and I will enrich the firmament with two stars, so that the stranded and confused being may be illumined.

Give me your vital string and I shall play notes of transfiguration.

77. Consciousness determines the space in which one lives.

The infinity of space-ether is equal to the infinity of the consciousness. The very moment one discovers the infinity of consciousness one comes into contact with spatial infinity too.

78. In order to hear a sound-wave you must placate your restless mental substance, otherwise you are not listening and your inner ear cannot be enraptured by any Harmony.

Unfortunately there are people who listen to music only with their physical senses while their mind-consciousness is elsewhere.

How can you possibly harmonize with spatial Infinity if you are always busy conceiving imperfections and disturbing sounds?

79. The incarnate vibrating string must be rendered mute and silent. And however difficult this may seem, you must achieve it if you wish to resonate a new "model of life" and perform a new dance of events.

On the other hand you have no choice: either you live in discordant conflict or you modulate your instrument to the sweetness of Beauty and the gentleness of Accord.

Harmony concedes itself to those who are capable of tuning their precious consciential harp beautifully.

80. Imagine less and play your harp more; this means that you must be Harmony rather than represent Harmony to yourself. Between imagining and *being* there runs an abyss, it is the difference between an aspirant musician and a Master musician.

81. I can wait because radiant Love-Accord does not know time. The power of Harmony resonates eternally upon the plane of non-resistance and offers itself to the traveller who lends his ear and his Heart.

82. Are you perhaps a Lover seeking for his *immortal* Beloved? Do you wish to be one with the Beloved of your heart who does not know Time and disperses the mists of space? I shall give you the sequences of that Work which will raise you up to the Summit of Beauty-Love in itself.

83. You must, first of all, *visualize* the image of your Beloved (*Iṣṭadevatā*, *Netjer*, the Master, *Avatāra*, etc.) at the Center of your heart. You must visualize him in his formal aspect, therefore with an exceptionally majestic body, the archetype of Beauty, emanating a radiant *sympathy*. You must, obviously, feel yourself deeply in tune with him. This ideal construction must be tended in every minute detail until it becomes a life-pulsating Being of marvelous beauty. Your way of proceeding must be calm and persistent; you must use a gentle enveloping, penetrating Fire. You must be in no hurry, but at the same time have a joyful determination that may allow you the possibility of keeping your mind from wandering away from your construction.

Forty-five minutes a day will be sufficient at first. Later you may reach an hour a day, and if you are more capable, you may reach two hours a day, but not consecutively.

During the day you must not waste your mental energies on useless conceptualizations and words. You must impose upon yourself a certain inner absorption in order to concentrate your fire and dominate it. You should also know that from the moment of your ascesis *you no longer belong to yourself.* You are conceding yourself *consciously*, and transfiguring yourself in your Beloved. Your *conscious* will must slowly retire to a point where you will call out: not mine but thy Will be done. What matters most is to do all this in a conscious way. It is not an *object* that concedes itself but an active living *subject*.

This creative meditation must last until the image appears naturally and spontaneously as a pure object of *contemplation*. When you have finished creating and you simply contemplate, then you may move on to another creative act. You must project *Divine qualities* and incorporate them into the image. The Quality may be: Intelligible Knowledge, Love-Beauty,

Spiritual Will, etc., The important thing is to transmit intelligible, universal, supra-individual Qualities to the image. This is of *utmost* importance for a number of reasons.

This creative meditation too must last until you are able to *contemplate* the incorporated Quality without any effort. At this point you have created a Being expressing Life-quality. Your *string* must resonate certainty, you must have complete dominion over yourself and a total absence of fear. You may thus contemplate your Beloved because he is before you full of splendor like the mid-day sun. Your condition must be *receptive* and, at the same time, you must pay attention to the *response* of your consciousness and psyche; this means opening up your "inner hearing". When you begin to notice a certain response to the "qualitative influence" of the Beloved (this means that you are manifesting the Note of your Beloved which, in its turn, implies a extremely *active* position on your side so as to transform your note into his), you can pass on to a fourth phase: shortening the distance between yourself and the image-quality until you merge with it.

At this stage you may drop your formal support and contemplate, assimilate and express – now at one with your Beloved – the pure Quality. This implies bringing yourself onto the pure vibratory plane of *identity* with your Beloved. The Lover-Beloved duality disappears and there subsists a unity of vibration-color of an indescribable power and beauty, above and beyond the formal aspect.

You are He, He is you.

And if by any chance your Beloved should be wearing a body, it will not be your bodies that attract each other, but the Qualities, or better still, the identity of color-vibration, the "elective affinity", the identity of "ray", the identity-unity of life, the identity of Beauty and of the splendor of Beauty.

84. Certainly you will admit the fact that a body-form represents only a "medium", a means, a simple instrument through which divine Qualities are revealed; they may be expressed in their intelligible purity, or may be degraded and impoverished by a non-purified individuality. Every body-volume is quantity, an inert compound which has no intrinsic reality of its own. Seen from a metaphysical point of view it is an illusion, an appearance, a non-being. Its function is simply that of transmitting Qualities, which are perennial realities since they belong to the world of Being.

The Soul is beautiful because its beauty is living, pulsating, dynamic, expressive, stimulating and exalting. The beauty of the body is static, without vitality and in itself is inexpressive. In fact it is the artist's task to give *life*, expression, or in other words, a *soul* to his creations. The human being, for example, cannot be defined exclusively in terms of its body; it is much more; it is will, intelligence, love, creativity, goodness, etc.

Now, if there must be union with your Beloved, this may take place only within the ambit of Quality-Reality and not within the dimension of appearance-quantity. The Beloved is, first and foremost, Love-Beauty, Warmth-Bliss; he is the very Archetype of Beauty. This is your Beloved; and if initially I advised you to create for him a body-form, this is only because I considered you – perhaps wrongly – incapable of fusing directly with the very essence of your Beloved.

But, in order to fuse with what is Beautiful, you must necessarily become Beautiful yourself.

Identity with the Beloved may occur only when your vibrant string becomes able to resonate *his* Note; then Accord produces fusion and synthesis, and Beauty shines in *unity* which is incommensurable completeness and ecstasy.

One might well say that Love – in the deepest sense – implies unity. A love which does not lead to unity is not love but only individualized sensorial desire, which involves mere duality. This is why you have been reminded often not to confuse desire with all-pervading Love and, in the same way, not to mistake simple erudition about phenomenal facts for noetic Knowledge, which must lead to identity with the object of knowledge, just as Love must lead to perfect unity with the Beloved.

The very force-energy of material and corporeal sex is a symbol of the demand for *unity*, but only a symbol because authentic unity can never be obtained upon the mere level of body-appearance, but only by means of *qualitative affinity*. What can unite you with your Beloved is not the body-volume which is mortal, relative, opaque and inexpressive, but only the revelation of Beauty, the sound of Love, the harmony of Bliss and the enchantment of ecstasy. A body-volume must be created (since it comes and goes), but Qualities, like Beauty, do not have to be created because they already exist and have always existed; you must simply reveal them. You who are the Lover of Beauty and of Love cannot but fuse and annul yourself in that which is Beautiful and the authentic expression of Love. However, and I insist upon this, you must not mistake the cause for the effect. Love Music, merge with Music, become Music, but do not fuse and identify with the musical instrument, be it a piano, a harp, a trumpet, etc. You would simply be asking for the impossible, the unachievable.

Remember that Qualities can also exist in their pure state without the intermediary of the material body, just as the Soul can exist even without the gross body. However, a body-form without life-Quality cannot subsist.

The majority – who do not love Beauty and who do not seek true Love – are inter-related at the level of body-appearance and so their union is an illusion that offers only opposition, dullness, conflict and formal, animal needs.

But you, Lover of Beauty, of Love and of the musical gentleness of Accord, having re-educated your vibrant string by means of transcendental aesthetics, you can rise above the perishable compound and enfold, in a transfiguring embrace, that Beauty-Love which triumphs over time and space[1].

Let me now remind you of the phases of the Work:

1. Creation-visualization of the Form of the Beloved.

2. Projection-visualization of the vital Quality.

3. Steady and uninterrupted contemplation of the Beloved such as to call forth a response from you. In this manner, on the one hand you make yourself *receptive*, on the other, intensely *active* so as to respond suitably to the vibrations of your Beloved. (You must admit the fact that one cannot love by word alone but by offering the *totality* of oneself transfigured into pure Beauty).

4. Drawing closer and closer to the Beloved until duality disappears.

5. Identity with the vibration-color of the Beloved.

6. Revelation of the sublime "dance" of Beauty.

---

[1] For a further comprehension of the Traditional Teaching of Love-Beauty see, Raphael, *The Science of Love*, and the Chapter "The Ascension of the Philosophical Eros" in, Raphael, *Initiation into the Philosophy of Plato*, Aurea Vidyā. New York.

III

COLORLESS FIRE

Realization according to Traditional Metaphysics

1. The two pathways described above are windows, frames that open out upon the Infinite; you may open them and leap into the sky that is not limited by any circumference.

The first pathway rests upon the qualification of Will-determination, upon solar Dignity; the second is based on æsthetic sensitivity, on love of the Beautiful, on inner hearing as the Pathway of ascesis. There are, naturally, other pathways, other windows that open wide upon the Bliss of the Infinite, and to follow one out of so many of them depends upon each individual's inclination.

There is also a particular pathway, one that is very special because it is not upon the plane of distances; on this path there are no frames, therefore one must leap suddenly out of the window and be able to remain in the unknown. Thus, all of a sudden you are deprived of all your supports, of all your body-vehicles and even of qualities. This pathway does not rest upon anything familiar, because you have to place yourself immediately beyond quantity, quality, cause and effect; that is, beyond time-space.

This is the path of the "arrow", the metaphysical pathway, the way of colorless Fire. In *Vedānta* one speaks of *asparśa* which means without relations, without contact, without supports or bases. It is not meant for all; on the contrary, it is for the very few who must tread carefully because it is easy to misconstrue things that do not rest upon conceptualization, emotion, will or action.

For the metaphysical pathway "non-pathway" you must possess intelligent daring, be prepared, and have particular prerequisites in order to avoid the risk of getting lost in "nothingness", of finding yourself, after leaving your window behind, being neither on the inside nor on the outside.

For example, if I say to you: «There is neither dawn or sunset, neither brightness or darkness», you might feel disoriented because for you these are *phenomena* as real as your corporeal consistency. But I am not speaking to you from an earthly point of view, which is your window, but from the point of view of the sun. This is the crucial point of this non-pathway: suddenly I speak a language which is not familiar to you, which is not yours. Now, will you be able to leave your terrestrial window, to do without supports and to throw yourself suddenly into the sun?

And again, if I say: «There exists neither birth nor dissolution, neither aspirant to liberation nor liberated, nor anyone who is in bondage...»[1], I think that you may be perplexed if you were unable to find the correct position of consciousness and make your empirical relational mind fall silent.

If you feel ready and you have the courage to cross the abyss, then with the sponge of "perfect Knowledge" you will learn how to remove immediately the million yesterdays that imprisoned you and obliged you to stay in the state of conflicting becoming. You do not combat the Dragon, you transcend it in one leap, integrating it. *Comprehension dissolves* the "monster" because you recognize it as mere appearance which can frighten only the non-knower.

---

[1] Gauḍapāda, *Māṇḍūkyakārikā*: II, 32. Translation from the Sanskrit and Commentary by Raphael, Aurea Vidyā, New York.

2. Know that metaphysics goes beyond the physical, the psychic and even the spiritual. Often some define what is simply psychological – or belonging to the subtle, "astral" or metapsychical plane – as metaphysical. It is necessary to point out right from the start that metaphysics is concerned with the ultimate Reality of things, the universal Constant, the Absolute or the Infinite which is *beyond time, space* and *cause.*

All that concerns the individual, and therefore the general, refers to science in the modern sense of the term; all that concerns the universal, the transcendental unity, the totality as the Cause of the cause of everything, refers to metaphysics.

3. The study of phenomena, movement, the relative, or the world of names and forms in all its extent and whatever the order, represents academic science, magical arts and Theurgy. The study of the noumenon, the motionless, the permanent, the absolute, the non-qualified, the non-formal, the invariable, the great Silence, constitutes metaphysics.

4. All that refers to the manifest (gross-physical and subtle or supra-physical) belongs to a general and formal order. Metaphysics goes beyond all science, profane as well as sacred, therefore it is not cosmology, or ontology, which refers to the One-principle. The metaphysical pathway in the *Qabbālāh* is the one leading to *Ain Soph*; in Alchemy is the way that leads to the solution of *Sulphur* itself; in *Vedānta* the way to *Nirguṇa* or *Turīya*. For Plato and Plotinus it is the realization of the One–Good, which transcends the very Being or One-Many.

5. If metaphysics is the quest for the Absolute and for Reality without a second, then it cannot be schematized, conceptualized or forced within certain individualized mental frames. The Absolute or the ultimate Reality cannot be circumscribed, represented or brought to the plane of an empirical relativism, nor can it be the exclusive property of an individual or of a people. If I speak to you of Oriental metaphysics and in particular of *Advaita Vedānta*, this does not depend upon the fact that it is Oriental, but because it is just metaphysics and, above all, *Traditional Metaphysics*[1].

6. All sciences have the mind and intuition of the sensorial order as their cognitive instruments, therefore they avail of indirect, mediated means of knowledge. Metaphysics uses as its cognitive instrument supraconscious, suprasensible intuition or pure reason, devoid of individualized sentimental or mental conditioning, therefore it operates by means of a direct and immediate perceptive instrument. To engage in metaphysics one needs a *mens informalis*[2].

7. The various sciences resort to a *method* of investigation to discover the laws that govern nature. Their sphere of action remains the infra-natural; the god of science might well be called nature.

Ontology tries to discover the first Cause or the "unmoved mover" that has caused nature or movement, therefore it is

---

[1] For further treatment of metaphysical ascesis, reference can be made to the following texts published by Aurea Vidyā in New York: Raphael, *Tat tvam asi* (That thou art), Śaṅkara, *Vivekacūḍāmaṇi* and, Raphael, *Initiation into the Philosophy of Plato*.

[2] Non-formal mind, i.e. the mind when not modified by idea-forms/projections; *buddhi* for *Vedānta*.

interested in the Being-principle or the One as the origin of the series.

Metaphysics goes beyond the *natural* and even beyond the first Cause, placing itself within the non-qualified state of Non-Being, as pure and absolute Being-without-a-second (Non-duality).

8. There are two classes of monists: the materialists or actualists and the spiritualists or essentialists. The former say that everything is matter or substance (in the strict sense) and, since matter-substance is perceivable only by means of the five senses and the mind, which synthesizes the data recorded by the senses, matter is a simple sensorial thing distinct from the sensorial subject. Without meaning to do so, this view opens the way to an irreducible dualism. The second school of monists maintains that all is spirit or essence and, as the spirit cannot be perceived by the five senses or by the empirical mind, it must be the object of faith.

This duality between spirit and matter and between empirical reason and faith, has caused many disputes, struggles and even bloodshed.

From a metaphysical point of view spirit and matter, essence and substance, subject and object, noumenon and phenomenon do not constitute an irreducible duality but a simple *polarity* which is in fact resolved in metaphysical unity, in the unconditioned, in the non-qualified infinite.

Only metaphysics can solve the problem of all manifest duality and therefore of all the struggles that can unfortunately derive from such dualistic points of view.

As already stated, in the East this metaphysical vision is called Non-duality (*Advaita*), while the name that is given by Platonism is One-One.

9. Thus, for the metaphysician all theories that stem from sensorial relations and from apperception are simple *points of view* which, when correlated to the synthetic or unifying vision of reality, represent partial truths and particular fragments of the universal mosaic.

The metaphysical vision not only *sees* the sensible or formal particular, not only *sees* the universal life-principle or the intelligible, but it goes further and reveals the supreme Reality (*parasat*). It is from Reality that both the world of forms and that of living beings draw their raison d'être; in other words, it goes beyond the sensorial and the intelligible.

10. The truth which we call scientific (in the modern sense of the word) is truth in its specific field of investigation. When we discover that a phenomenon behaves in a certain way and may have a particular field of application, we state a true thing; but this represents only a degree of truth, not the total Reality. Not only that, but some phenomenal truths may be contradicted in time and annulled by other phenomenal truths.

To depend exclusively upon phenomenal truth means not only precluding the discovery of the universal Truth, or the constant, from which all fluctuating phenomena draw their origin, but it also means putting the human being in reductive, mutilated, and one-sided terms, thus causing his alienation and conflict.

If we were to depend only on sensorial perception we could never reach constant and sure knowledge: the sensorial phenomena are contingent and changing. Now, the fleeting existence of phenomena, being potency-act, cause-effect, and therefore movement, must necessarily rest upon something stable, uncaused, a true reality; it must presuppose a moving

Principle, able to act, and an unmoved Principle, which has its own being in itself, and which shows itself to be pure act, *causa sui* [self-caused], pure knowledge, and not a fluctuating, uncertain and contradictory opinion.

The mobility of things and of sensorial entities produces a knowledge which is mobile, modifiable and fleeting.

And do some not say that truth can be invented and that it may last but a single season?

11. There are also the followers of *scientism* (not true scientists) who vigorously propose that whatever cannot be perceived through the senses must be rigorously banned from research and knowledge. The truth is that the egos of these followers of scientism create defense mechanisms, as they have an *a priori* attachment to the philosophical conception that all must be phenomena. If one were to remove the ideological scaffolding which this ego has constructed for itself and upon which it obviously rests, it would certainly collapse and find itself in a condition of void.

The individual and even the "genius" is often a dogmatist, a theologian or a systematic philosopher. For the metaphysician such an individual is a child who is afraid of being disturbed while playing with his material, phenomenal and fleeting toys.

12. Etymologically the word "philosophy" comes from *philos* = friend, and *sophia* = wisdom-knowledge, and therefore it means friend of knowledge-wisdom. But over time the word philosophy has come to mean friend of individual, empirical and representational reason. Today – generally speaking – philosophy debates are based on *mental representations*. For a long time now, philosophy has become

the empirical, logical-rational and systematic conception of a certain individual and often is not experienced even by its creator.

Even for Aristotle *to know is to be* because true knowledge must generate authentic catharsis within an individual. Whoever seeks mental representations alone obviously remains what he is.

Traditional Philosophy (please allow us to use the capital letter) leads to *realization*. It is cathartic and transforming because, as Plato holds, it represents a means of *ascesis*.

One who does not live Knowledge does not know; if Knowledge does not become consciousness it is not authentic Knowledge but simple memory of data and cognition of facts. It is necessary to insist on the fact that for a traditional society, Knowledge must resolve itself into awareness of being. In such a society, knowledge of an exclusively accumulative and quantitative order, perpetuating dualism and therefore all possible aporias, is not conceivable.

13. For a metaphysical realization one needs beyond doubt, certain qualifications of consciousness, but also an intellect capable of transcending the temporal. The majority are constrained by space-time and for them it is difficult to emerge from it, but if one wishes to realize Metaphysical Knowledge one must be able to *fly*. This, though, does not mean losing oneself in the simple "indefinite", in vagueness and approximation.

14. To grasp the atemporal in its immediacy means not to depend upon any psycho-physical practice. It means sinking all of a sudden into the all-inclusive and all-pervading Present. Metaphysical realization occurs *hic et nunc* (here and now).

To speak of epochs and temporal cycles or of the passing of races and civilizations etc., means discussing time-space and therefore history; a historiographical conception of life remains materialistic, therefore relative and phenomenal. But it must be said that there are also "spiritualists" who, paradoxically, are materialists.

15. Thus, some spiritualistic doctrines remain locked in time-space, although they speak of absolute truth, that is metaphysical truth. Perhaps their authors are not aware of what a "metaphysical vision" implies, although metaphysics is not a vision in the usual sense.

One must acknowledge that metaphysics belongs to an *élite*, not because of supranatural reasons but because there are very few who are able to *fly* and are tending to break all circumferences and barriers. Those who love freedom, the true and authentic freedom of Being-without-a-second are very few indeed. The majority seeks the Divine or the supranatural as a simple mental outlet, for psychological comfort or as a protection of the empirical ego. When they do not find these things they try to adapt and put themselves at the service of phenomenal or of *ideological systems*, be these philosophical, political-economic, religious, etc., thus taking the road to alienation.

The metaphysician does not *preserve* his individuality but he *transforms* it, by resolving it. To say it with *Vedānta*, the metaphysician is not a Viṣṇuite (preserver of the world of names and of forms, therefore of space-time) but Śaivaite (transformer and resolver of the world of names and forms). This also implies that the metaphysician transcends or resolves multiplicity into unity. Thus the metaphysical vision is one of synthesis, wholeness, unity and essence, because the way of synthesis (not of syncretism) is the pathway to solution, reintegration and true initiation.

16. Metaphysics belongs to the *Greater Mysteries* because it represents supreme Knowledge (*paravidyā*) while science, in all its indefinite possibilities of application, belongs to the *Lesser Mysteries*, because it is knowledge of the physical and the psychical (*aparavidyā*). The cosmological and the psychological do not represent the *Greater Mysteries*. The majority are inclined toward secondary or non-supreme knowledge because the instrument of cognition, being of a sensorial nature, is easier for them.

17. To arrive at a metaphysical vision of reality means placing oneself at the Pole, at the central Point, the hub of the wheel; it means getting to the center of the cross. The mean way is neither right nor left, yet it is not even at the center in the normal sense, because the mean way is that supreme Point where polarities are resolved and completely transcended.

18. When they are considered independently, religion – as this term is normally intended – dogmatic theology, empirical philosophy, science in its physical and psychical dominion and occultism in the broadest sense etc., have nothing to do with metaphysics.

These disciplines may, however, be considered as being developments of the Principle, particular aspects or modalities of metaphysics. Their raison d'être and their significance can make sense if they are subjected to the Principle.

Traditionally, sacred Science (astrology, cosmology, sacred magic, psychology, etc.) was derived from the metaphysical vision, and when the metaphysical vision was lost, at least to the majority, sacred Science became profane; by excluding the metaphysical vision it lost its sacred function and its true raison d'être.

When the sole knowledge is divided, broken up, fragmented and every little fragment claims total truth for itself, it falls into illusion and into error. A civilization cannot but fail when the central Sun of knowing fails, because it becomes fragmentary, in opposition and in conflict.

If the ultimate truth of things is of an essential, noumenal, simple, universal and constant order, then only metaphysics dares grasp the Reality without a second.

19. To speak of metaphysical truth is one thing, to *be* that truth is quite a different matter. The majority like to speak because this simply requires a slight vocal effort.

There are others who speak of metaphysics because they have the gift of evasion. One must reflect and convince oneself that traditional metaphysics is realization, and realization means freedom from all that is sensorial or intelligible.

But who truly loves the integral solution of one's own incompleteness? There are, without doubt, many *paṇḍits*, theologians and scholars of the sacred sciences: they carry out their *dharma*, but very few are capable, in the silence of their own hearts, of striking the fatal blow that destroys *avidyā* (metaphysical ignorance).

20. In conclusion, metaphysics rests upon itself, as it is based upon the absoluteness of the Principle; therefore, it cannot depend on any particular science or knowledge, which are interested only in the ever changing *nature* in general.

From this stems the fact that the metaphysical vision escapes all definition, all schemes and all particularisms.

21. If Love is the accord of polarities, annulment of distances, a harmony capable of resolving the opposites and the eurythmy of the whole, then the metaphysician is that being who most concretely reveals the Love and Harmony of the spheres.

22. There is an action produced by the empirical ego and an action generated by the metaphysical harmonic Center. The former is the outcome of appropriation, utilitarianism, egoistic vision, greed and attachment to things-events; the latter is the fruit of a universal vision which grants fullness and completeness.

In the former there are tensions, conflicts, jarring noise and resistance, in the latter there is relief from tensions, expansion, silence and radiant Love.

The former operates upon the plane of effort, mass and condensed Fire, the latter upon the plane of permeability, synthesis and radiant Fire. The former acts to accumulate and separate, creating disharmony within the vital unity, the latter acts to unify, integrate and pacify.

23. Egoistical passions unleash shattering and mortifying sounds, but in order not to abandon his disturbing passions the individual constrains himself within bondage and pain. The gifts of Immortality and then of Eternity, which tower above the virgin substance, will be given to those who are able to attain them.

24. True meditation of the heart is *comprehension*. To comprehend we must transform our mind using the power of Fire. Metaphysical knowledge is a "Fire that consumes".

25. There can never be a social law, however perfect, capable of producing a right relationship among beings. Every piece of legislation, which is born of *individuality*, is a simple palliative, created to satisfy certain contingent needs.

The true solution to the matter of a "right relationship", at every level and degree, is to be found in following the metaphysical way or vision; this is the only way capable of placing the individual under the law of the universal. A perfect State is one which is commensurate with the Principle. The State proposed by Plato is a perfect one because it is commensurate with the metaphysical vision of life.

26. If realization is Union and, at higher levels, *identity* with the Principle-without-a-second, then the metaphysician is able to reveal the highest form of Realization known.

27. Nothing can be added to or taken away from what *is*. To add to or subtract (plus-minus) from something which has always been, is and always will be, is equivalent to considering the Absolute as lacking in fullness, in wholeness and in bliss.

28. «The immortal cannot become mortal, nor the mortal become immortal because there cannot be a change in nature»[1].

---

[1] Gauḍapāda, *Māṇḍūkyakārikā*, The Metaphysical Path of Vedānta: III, 21. Op.cit.

29. «How can a man, who believes that a being which is immortal by nature can become mortal, at the same time maintain that the immortal, which is produced (manifested), can retain its immortal nature?»[1].

30. «The dualists affirm the birth of the non-born. But how can that which is Non-born and immortal become mortal?»[2].

31. «It is by virtue of *māyā* – with the exclusion of every other possibility – that this Non-born (*Brahman* without a second) may differentiate itself. If the differentiation were real, then the immortal would become mortal»[3].

32. «As long as there is mental representation of causality, the endless wheel of birth and death continues to turn. But when the thought of causality is resolved, then birth and death cease to be produced»[4].

33. If the world of phenomena is continual change, unceasing transformation and simple appearance, can the Permanent, the Eternal, the Immortal and the absolutely Constant ever be found there?

34. How can there be temporal discontinuity, evolution and cycles of birth and death in the Eternal present?
    The Eternal present means Indivisibility, which necessarily excludes all fragmenting, composition or becoming.

---

[1] *Ibid.*: III, 22
[2] *Ibid.*: III, 20
[3] *Ibid.*: III, 19
[4] *Ibid.*: IV, 56

One cannot conceive of a God who *becomes*, who is born
and dies, who shrinks and grows, who ascends and descends.

35. «It is not possible to state, in fact, that something
real reaches existence; nor is it possible to say that a vessel
that is non-existent in this moment becomes existent the following moment because this would be the same as stating
a contradiction. As soon as we realize that things have no
absolute existence, we also realize that they cannot produce
other things possessing such existence.

Thus, when we speak of causes we go against logic;
we actually indulge in the expedients of subject and object,
substance and attributes, space and time; but, in the absolute
sense, there is neither cause nor effect, neither generation
nor termination»[1].

36. Totality or Unity can only be *divided* logically.
Quantitative multiplicity of the Being is a simple opinion
invented for ease of reference for the ego.

37. If the Absolute is without cause and without movement, then what kind of cause and movement might the
Liberated promote? If the things you perceive in yourself
and outside of yourself *are not* – because they belong to
the sphere of the contingent and the fleeting, which is non-
being – tell me: what must you detach yourself from? If you
comprehend and are the unique and perfect Reality without
a second, tell me, in whom can you base your expectations
or of whom should you be afraid?

---

[1] S. Radhakrishnan: *Indian Philosophy*, Vol. I, pag. 665, Edizioni Aśram
Vidyā, Rome. (Italian Edition).

If the sword of intellective *discernment* (*Noûs*) reveals Truth as unique and undivided Reality, tell me, how can you still see the world of error and opinion?

If the blazing sun shines in you, tell me, how can you still see darkness?

38. Things-events or time-space do not lead to the unconditioned Being. When things-events or time-space cease to exist, Being reveals and shows itself effortlessly.

39. It is not desire but the ending of desire that leads to non-desire.

It is not thought but the ending of thinking that leads to non-thought.

It is not ignorance but the ending of ignorance that leads to knowledge.

40. «Thus, real development, which is nothing but integration, appears to him as successions – History – or as self representation – Philosophy – or as a yearning – Religion. The first one by fixing mobility which cannot be reduced to succession, the second by crystallizing immutability which cannot be reduced to immobility, and the last one by making a parody of certainty which cannot be reduced to promise. So, by turning toward that which can never be, the human being breaks himself off and loses himself. Illusory knowledge is opposed by an equally illusory action, to a whirlwind without center is opposed a purposeless agitation: what is lost in the domain of life is what has become crystallized and established as a fictitious being in the domain of knowledge. The human being is a child born at midnight – states a Taoist text – who believes that yesterday never existed: empty on the inside,

the breath has withdrawn from him. Pushed from without he is turned toward the outside. Thus modern human being falls under the dazzling of the future, never suspecting, in his poorness, what he does not see what exceeds him, what is *before* him and what is *behind* him as a deep and invisible vein. When the rhythm of Contemplation is exhausted, the pace of Action is increased artificially.

History, art, philosophy, belief – amid these four corpses the being-corpse lives out the myth of the future, that is the unrealizable, and he makes of them the crown and the mask at his own death: dead before birth he claims a life to come: putrefied before living, he plays in agony with a future resurrection: in an empty present he turns toward an illusory advent»[1].

41. Time is the Eternal, the Immortal seen from the fragmentary view-point of mental perception. There are various levels of perception of time which, when all is said and done, mutually exclude each other. The "time" of one subject under certain circumstances is different from the "time" of another subject. Time is a relational truth, therefore it is a relative truth, a truth of representation.

42. Are you perhaps interpreting Reality in terms of the "beginning of time" and of the "ending of time"?

Come now, there is nothing worse than becoming attached to fleeting and phenomenal phantoms, nor is there greater foolishness than believing in the non-existent.

---

[1] From: *Introduzione alla Magia*, Vol. II, Ch. III. Edited by the "Ur Group", Edizioni Mediterranee. Rome. (Italian edition).

If you want the *certainty* of your being do not hope
in, nor pursue time-images. Do not believe in that security
which time, like a human tale, offers you; time can only
offer you illusion and conflict.

Your *certainty* lies in without-time, in that time which
does not become, because it is the "eternal now".

43. In order to live, you, who do not grasp a-temporality
or the eternal present, have created for yourself a God of
"becoming", a God that walks and bounces. The psychological
ego is capable of anything, even of creating a hop-scotching
God for himself.

44. Liberation does not occur in time; if you speak of
time, you are in bondage.

But to escape from time means to leave the sensorial-
conceptual frame, and this gives the shudders to whoever
thinks of himself as thought.

If you go on placing yourself within time, you will no
doubt find yourself in time; by "going" you will not reach
your goal.

45. Wherever there is time, there is space, as together
they represent your *need* and your metaphysical ignorance.
Time gives you hope, and space comfort, but these things
belong to the empirical ego, not to the Self. If you love
the empirical ego then lull yourself in time and space; if
you love the Self then dare and "kill" the serpent that bites
its own tail.

46. Time means "beginning" and beginning means
"death". Birth and death are correlated with time. But a

thing that already exists cannot be born and a thing that has never existed cannot come into existence. The Eternal cannot be born and that which is not eternal has no substantial reality.

Time leads into time. If you cling to impermanent becoming thinking that you can transcend your incompleteness, you will discover at the end of all the temporal cycles that you are still exactly at the point of departure. You will not find the solution to becoming in the becoming-process-history.

In time and with time you will not be able to quench your thirst for liberation.

Flee from those who profess themselves the adorers of time.

If you have chosen, then there is only one road: that of Fire, of the Lightning Bolt, of the Dart.

47. Oh you who travel on embers of Fire resist the ascending flame until you see time reduced to ashes.

The personification of becoming is an objectification in which truth is hidden.

Time wants to make a slave of man, as does history in all its various ramifications.

Victory over these historical phantoms is creative strength, and creative activity releases liberty and wholeness.

48. Either you are relativity, and therefore you must resign yourself to living in conflicting dualism, or you are Absoluteness and therefore you live your constant and the One without a second. To be what you are you do not have to ask leave of anyone.

If you say that you are one and the other, I tell you that this is not possible because these two factors exclude one another reciprocally. Light contradicts darkness and the latter contradicts the former, life contradicts death and death contradicts life.

If you tell me that you are *also* relativity then I answer that for you this relativity is simply an accident, a mere passing phenomenon which, confronted with your absolute-ness, has null value.

49. Either you are mortal, and in this case count your days of misery, or you are immortal and then life can acquire a real sense for you.

If you are mortal, this world which you have built and are building for yourself is just as mortal, therefore to what end should you build castles on the sand? Why act if its aim or goal are that of not being?

If you are mortal to what end love and serve phantoms that stink of carrion?

If you are mortal to what end beget children that no sooner are born than they are already swallowed up by the jaws of mortality and of annihilation?

50. If you are immortal why do you insist on living in a precarious state that does not belong to you?

If you are immortal then live and express your eternity; if you are immortal, then life and conscious beings are also immortal and therefore it is folly to try to transform, trans-mute or revolutionize what is immortal. There is nothing to be transformed, no-one to be redeemed or saved; it is just a question of eventually awakening sleeping beings to their immortality.

Immortality implies completeness, permanence, non-dependence, non-desire, non-activism and non-purpose. What could he who was never born and who can never die possibly desire, do or have?

The immortal is outside of time-space-cause, and whoever is outside of phenomenal transience lives of his own motion, he is *causa sui*, he is beyond process, beyond change, beyond producing.

51. If you awaken to your a-temporal, a-spatial, a-causal immortality, then you will solve all your existential problems at once; in truth your problems are not solved, they simply vanish like mist in the wind. Problems exist only in the contingency of becoming, but in the a-temporal there are no problems just as in the sun the dualistic problem of dawn and sunset does not exist.

52. What must we do to awaken to what we really are?

If you are a human being, and if thanks to your capacity to think and project freely, you believe yourself to be a tree, what must you do to consider yourself a human being once more? You need someone who, having *recognized* himself as a human being, stimulates you to become aware of the fact that you are a human being and not a tree.

And if you ask me: if I do not awaken even when receiving the proper stimulus, what may happen to me? Nothing, you do not cease for this reason to be an immortal being; however much you may believe yourself to be what you are not, you cannot change the true nature or what you really are. A belief is a belief, an opinion, a simple mental representation, and an opinion which does not move anything or produces nothing and alters nothing. Although the opinions of the world of men clash to the point of extreme folly, nonetheless they cannot change or alter anything. The being of belief and opinion, has always been a fanatic, a sectarian or a madman: that is what he is and will always be, despite technological "progress".

53. If you are really tired of sleeping in the world of beliefs-opinions, then you have nothing left to do but to awaken to your immortal and integral nature. Awareness alone – but total, integral awareness – is sufficient; do not ask for anything else. And as for those who still wish to sleep, let them sleep; this is their right.

Let the sleepers bury their sleepers and, as far as you are concerned, wake up to the awareness of your Eternity.

54. Therefore, if you dare rend with your discerning sword all that is a "second" or is other than yourself, then you will fix yourself in what you are and you will recognize yourself as being *pure Consciousness without content* or a second.

Remember: that image that appears to you in the mirror is not you, it is only the distorted reflection of what you are; your present knowledge refers to that image; it is indirect, reflected knowledge.

True knowledge is your very self, because there is only one reality and that is You. There are not, therefore, two realities: yours and that in the mirror (duality); the one in the mirror is not real, it is simply a distorted image, a reflection, a copy, an apparent second, a shadow. The movement of the image in the mirror is caused by the mirror, it is not you who is moving. What you see in the mirror, the second you, does not in reality exist, it has no beingness, it is an illusion produced by the mirror.

Remove your attention from the image and fix it upon the Subject, which is you. By withdrawing from the world of names and forms – to whatever dimension or degree they may belong – you will reveal yourself in all your stable Bliss and the second will vanish.

55. On the other hand, reflect. Being, in that it is – and it cannot but be – cannot become. Becoming, in that it becomes, can never Be.

As already mentioned, if a thing is Real then it cannot come into existence because it already *is*; if, on the other hand, it is not Real, then of necessity it cannot be within existence. A Reality which becomes is not conceivable because it would be subject to growth and diminution, to birth and death. And the non-real, having no beingness of its own, cannot consider itself as a datum in the absolute sense.

And what is it that you perceive and see? All you see, from the point of view of Being, is apparent movement which is a question of lines, planes and volumes that *appear* and *disappear*, that are and are not and that come and go. What value can you give to that which is and yet is not or to that which appears and then disappears? If you look for a moment at the sun reflected in moving water you will notice that it is not the sun that moves but the water which, due to its particular nature, is subject to becoming-movement. However, a non-knower might think that it is not the water which moves but the reflected sun. Thus, it is not Being which moves but its matter-substance-χώρα, to say it with the divine Plato, that in turn reflects different representations of Reality.

If therefore things are not because they are not Being, you must agree that to linger upon or allow oneself to be limited by or to submit oneself to data that appear and disappear is madness. So, you must distinguish Being from absolute non-being, and from that which, although participating in Being, is not Being. Now, if you are a seeker of the ultimate Reality or of the sole and one Reality – because there cannot be more than one Reality – you must recognize that the sole and authentic Reality is Being, and that everything posterior to It is not, and can never be.

Besides, if knowing a truth implies accepting it, and this is even more so in the case of *the* Truth, then you must agree that you cannot but *live* and *be* that Truth. And if the world of opinions proposes error to you, how could you, who at last have come to know and accept truth, contradict and disown yourself by changing sides?

In truth, you have only one road to follow, that of Being, leaving the sophisms of opinion to the world of men who believe themselves to be "becoming"[1].

---

[1] For the Way that leads to the Being, see: Parmenides, *On the Order of Nature*, Edited by Raphael, Aurea Vidyā. New York.

SECTION TWO

I

NON-DESIRE

1. An authentic polar position implies absence of desire. Pure consciousness is absence of emotional-mental content; it is a limpid and clean screen without superimposed images, precipitates or a second; it is pure Fire.

2. The Fire of joy emerges when all desires are resolved, when the conflicting ego is transcended. Thus, true joy is impersonal, beyond all emotional exuberance which is "water" in motion.

When you experience perfect Joy you are no longer yourself as empirical ego: there is only Joy that imposes Beauty upon space.

3. The activity of the common individual is made up of *reactions*, which are expressions of his particular individualized constitution. He is an "ego" surrounded by pleasant or unpleasant, attractive or repulsive objects, and the way he acts is the result of his desires, his fears and his past. Thus, all of his reactions are false, partial and inadequate because they are based on the egoistical foundation characterized by separateness.

One who is perfectly Realized enters the ego-less, desire-less state, where all reactive fires disappear; this determines an action which is impersonal, spontaneous, innocent and genuine.

4. A satisfied desire represents nothing but its own death.

When you thirst for happiness you are simply seeking the death of your very desire. This means that your truest desire is precisely non-desire, which appears to your consciousness as mere emptiness. And yet in this very emptiness you can discover the true nature of that beatific, pure and radiant Fire which cannot be quenched by water.

5. In the state of *non-desire* one asks for nothing; it represents absolute Fullness and Peace. It is the flow of Life with no ego in opposition, like the flight of the swallow in its perfect immobility or the beauty of a dawn which grants silence to the mind or the stillness of the waveless sea.

6. Desire is becoming and in becoming there is no Silence, love or attention; there is no yielding, no contemplation or revelation of the Essence.

When a desire arises this means that you are not at peace with yourself; in other words you are not *fixed* in yourself.

What is this restlessness which yearns and desires? What is that which disturbs?

Desire is centripetal fire, a state of anxiety; its gratification and weariness. It is the illusion of a moment.

7. It is not wise to strive to be different from what you are. It is not in the imitation of or in the identification with someone that you can find yourself.

You must dare to grasp your immortality in a silence in which you are absolutely alone, without the desire to be this or that, because "this" or "that" belong to the substance-matter-χώρα sphere which is continuously changing, and as such implies non-being.

8. To know the nature of desire is to reveal the origin of the acquiring and separating ego. It means knowing the totality of condensed fires.

This requires a rare attention focused on the process of mental exteriorisation and on reactions to things. Such attention is pure observation.

9. To transcend desire means having comprehended its real nature.

Until you find your ontological I, your non-formal Fire, you will be urged by desire from one object-event to another. But wanting to eliminate desire is already a desire; you cannot chase one illusion with another illusion.

It is when your consciousness dwells in the imponderable, in that state devoid of objectifying content, that desire loses its strength with all its ensnaring fascination.

The mind becomes pure and calm when it comprehends its movement, and comprehension is integration.

10. The mind projects the empirical ego, which repre-sents the experiencer-subject, and the picture-event, which becomes the object. This duality is alive as long as one identifies with the ego, which is a simple product, or with the object – which is deforming illusion – or with both which are process and becoming. This duality vanishes when the

mind resolves itself in the unity without a second. So, when dreaming, the mind projects the ego-experiencer (of dreams) and what is experienced. Such duality can be resolved only... by awakening from dream-desire.

The Awakened is one who has transcended all duality-polarity at the waking, dreaming and deep sleep levels, in other words, he has transcended the entire manifest fire-phenomenon.

11. Psychoanalysis aims at stabilizing the ego-desire because it considers it legitimately real. But stability cannot be given to that (the ego) which is born already fragmented and in conflict.

We cannot give sight to a blind person nor wisdom to a stone. The ego is a simple phenomenon, a continuity-discontinuity devoid of absolute reality, it is the reflection of the sun on water.

The "Pathway of Fire" leads to the transcendence and the resolution of that very ego-desire, the cause of endless divisions, unbalances and conflicts.

12. You must distinguish between radiant Joy or divine Bliss, and sensory and reflected happiness.

The former emerges from *absence of ego-desire*, the latter from an attractive reaction of egocentricity. The former is universal and everlasting; the latter is individual, exclusive and momentary.

13. If you wish to transcend desire, soften the dry Sun and the liquid Moon by means of the action of Fire until the

two are joined in the thalamus of your "vessel". Then you will obtain a glorious body that will be able to fly like an Eagle.

14. *"I* am happy" is a concept without sense. It presupposes a perceiving subject, a quality (happiness) and an object-event acting as the instrument of happiness. All this implies the creation of duality, but it is not upon the plane of duality that you can find the true Fire of the Philosophers; this emerges when subject-object and quality disappear from the screen of your consciousness.

15. It is the oblivion of the authentic Mercury of the Philosophers that gives rise in you to an outward-going desire-urge for happiness and wholeness; however, it remains without fruit because true radiant Joy can only be revealed by all-pervading Fire and can be regained at any moment of your existence.

16. There are many scholars who study problems concerning initiation and others full of esoteric cognitions: they are all impelled by desire.
The Realized ones are few because very few have the courage to face their inner enemy which is made up of fleeting intellectual-emotional *enjoyment.*

17. In desire there are incompleteness, restlessness and bewilderment. The common person cannot think of living without desires; the Sage does not resort to desire in order to act.

The Self simply reveals itself, innocently, naturally and freely. Though revealing itself the Self does not act and while manifesting itself it remains transcendent.

18. True inner Silence emerges not from inhibition of the empirical ego, but from a comprehension of the energies that cause the agitation of that ego. The majority of thought-desires derive from an unconscious mechanism of self-defence and from psychological fear of death. Desire is the force that drives one toward the peak of pain; desire cannot be quenched by continuing to desire.

19. Four questions must stimulate your consciousness:

1. What am I thinking about?
2. How do I think?
3. Why do I think-desire?
4. Who is it that thinks and desires?

If you ponder deeply upon these four points you will reveal the nature of the thinking subject, that of thought, the mechanism which urges you to think, the aim of your living-thinking. Only then will you be able to devote yourself to smoothing your rough stone.

20. «The human being is made in such a way that as soon as he has satisfied a desire another one arises as strongly as the previous one to stimulate him; and so he is kept perpetually in movement, nor can he ever achieve intimate satisfaction»[1].

---

[1] F. Galliani. *Letters*.

21. «We are never farther from our desires than when we imagine we possess desire»[1]. Desire is a mirage which creates never-ending motion, and drives us along a road without an outlet.

22. The range of desires is unlimited and is like a ladder: the higher you climb the more dissatisfied you become.

Desire is the cause of becoming; only the Fire of the Philosophers is capable of burning it.

23. «Like all men, I have desired honour and wealth and many times I have achieved more than I ever desired or hoped, and nonetheless I have never found within myself the satisfaction that I had imagined. Upon reflection, this is a sufficiently strong reason to remove a lot from the vain greed of men»[2].

24. When desire ceases, the wealth of the earth will be replaced by Bliss without object. True freedom is not social or political freedom, but the freedom that releases from desire and sensorial yearning that lives of the past.

25. Non-desire leads you to non-resistance, to absence of effort, to mental quietness, to detachment and to dis-identification from condensed or individualized Fire.

26. When all desires cease within the heart, the mortal recovers Immortality and all circumferences are resolved in the Point without dimension.

---

[1] J. W. Goethe, *Elective Affinities*.

[2] F. Guicciardini. *Civil and Political Memoirs*.

Flight upon the level of non-resistance belongs to a Soul that has resolved itself into *Ether.*

27. There are those who desire material wealth and others who desire celestial wealth. The motive does not change. It is always a question of gratifying a desire, and it is well known that desires are disparate and unforeseeable, but desire does not solve the existential problem.

28. Love cannot emerge when there is desire. To Love one must not desire; to Love-comprehend one must bring oneself to an attention without effort, without translatory motion. In desire there is possession, exclusion and death of the relationship. In desire and with desire there is no fruitful dialogue.

29. What you call love is really only desire. Truthfully, humanity has never been happy because it has simply desired and so you may come to the conclusion that Love does not represent bliss. This is the usual mistake of superimposition; that is, you have superimposed desire-conflict upon Love-Bliss, «mistaking the snake for the rope».

30. The more you desire the more you stray away from the fixation of the Mercury. The more you experience greed, the more you enter into illusion; the more you surround yourself with illusions, the less you will be able to reveal the incorruptible Sulphur. The "Pathway of Fire" consists in being able to break all limits, even those offering contentment.

31. If desire is not the solution to the problem of existence, then you must turn your attention to that state of consciousness which lives of its own motion, rests upon itself and offers silence and *pax profunda*. The authentic state of Being is freedom; freedom from desire, from having, from possessing, from taking.

Remember: pure Sulphur does not yield to those who are enslaved by earthly desire. If you do not kill the constraining Dragon with the sword or the spear, you will not be able to separate and sublimate your shining Body of glory.

II

SUPERIMPOSITION

1. There are a screen and a movie projected onto the screen. Often the individual identifies with the film of becoming and therefore with superimposition. The Liberated merges with the screen always identical to itself, beyond time and space; this implies that he reintegrates in the essence of Fire.

2. The majority superimpose the illusions-images-objects of the film upon the reality of the screen. This is the origin of metaphysical ignorance which makes them fall into conflict. To mistake illusions-images for absolute Reality is the condition of the non-awakened. To mistake the mere fleeting fires of the gross body, or the subtle or the causal one for the Self is the cause of bewilderment and suffering.

3. You ignore your authentic nature because you identify with your body, emotions and thoughts; superimpositions do not allow you to see the central Fire which is pure Sulphur. But when you find this Fire again, your perceptions, thoughts and emotions appear as simple movements of the empirical mind, like the waves and the ripples on the ocean, which you can fix or dissolve.

4. "Yesterday you were happy, today you are no longer so." What has happened to cause this difference?

You have simply superimposed the reaction-quality called unhappiness upon the substratum-consciousness, and the ego of the moment has identified itself with that quality believing itself to be either unhappy or happy.

We usually attribute qualities to a substratum which is indeed beyond quantities and qualities. We give the color-quality blue to the sky which in reality is colorless.

5. The individual creates his own reality of things, the fruit of his restless imagination.

One *imagines* the world now this way, now that way, but the underlying reality escapes him.

One *imagines* above and below, beautiful and ugly, just and unjust, but reality remains hidden all the time. Only when he ceases to imagine and superimpose will this ultimate reality be able to reveal itself.

The Real is infinite and we – simple contingent egos – cannot contain it. We can only let ourselves be taken and absorbed. Fire must devour fire.

6. The eternal present is the particular state peculiar to the birthless Self.

From the point of view of the Self, the universe of names and forms represents an expansion and contraction, an appearance and disappearance. With this awareness one grasps the entire process, one recognizes the magic of being and non-being, the workings of that which we call phenomena.

7. The eternal present cannot be placed into any category of the past or of the future. Reality is *hic et nunc*. Thus it remains extraneous to all mental frames and so it is inexpressible; it can only be understood by realizing it. It is the substratum-screen: it is from it that the indefinite fires emerge when they slowly condense; it is to it that they return when they dissolve.

8. True existence is established when the consciousness is free of contents-objects. Such consciousness, being non-formal Fire, escapes all qualification.

The best definition we can give of it is: deep and unspeakable peace. It is our Gold in its pure state.

9. To realize that peace, one must eliminate the categories of vulgar Mercury, that is to say, all deforming superimpositions. One must live in a state of deep "attention without tension", a state of extreme rarefaction, where shadows and light fade away, dissolving in the splendor of all-pervading Fire.

10. The Awakened knows neither birth nor death, cause or effect, neither waking, dreaming or deep sleep. The Awakened is beyond time, space and cause because he has been able to shatter all those conceptual superimpositions and recognize the Identity of all that really is. From this perspective, supreme Consciousness coincides with Being.

11. The concepts of immanence and transcendence, of above and below, lower and upper, profane and sacred, matter and spirit, etc., are nothing but superimpositions upon the Being that *is*. When all these mental categories are eliminated,

the individual is left without his ideal playthings and lives in a state of imponderability that could well be frightening. But illusions cannot but disappear sooner or later. All that belongs to the saṁsāric Dragon must be transcended.

12. Outside of the imperishable Self, all knowledge is simply knowledge of "objects". The Self can therefore be known only in a non-dual way. The ontological I reveals itself as being conscious of its own fullness. Fire recognizes itself as power to free and bind. We can know the object of knowledge, never the being as the ultimate transcendent Subject. This, as self-shining Fire, reveals itself by itself because it is *causa sui*.

13. When the consciousness of an individual is turned completely toward the absolute essence of Fire, the mind abandons all its perceptive finite contents; the vital energetic activity is reoriented and the being subsists alone, in its own *light* of glory.

14. Erudition is learned ignorance, a fleeting fire. It superimposes itself upon the real, veiling it continuously. Many do not love reality but only erudition, which represents a quantitative description of changing phenomena.

15. The human being has created the concept of time-space in order to be able to crystallize and perpetuate his body, his home, his ambitions, his honours and his egoistical thirst for power. But there exists only the bare and essential resonance of universal sound, which bursts forth as the Fire of being, devoid of contents, immobility, time-space and causality.

16. It is within the Reality-principle that you can find the motion revolving around its own axis. In becoming, you will find only a type of elliptical translatory motion and identification with substance. Your aspiration to grasp the Absolute, although justified, may take the wrong direction. It is not by change that you can attain the *immobile center*, it is not through processes that you can stop time.

17. If your mind lives in perfect peace and if none of your subconscious schemes are superimposed upon your entire consciousness forcing you to experience pseudo feeling and knowledge, then your vibrations will be in harmony with Being. But if your mind forces its own process, then you will be discordant music and shattering and mortifying sound.

18. A reiterated mental movement produces a habit and this, in turn, leads to limitation and bondage. One must not crystallize oneself into habits that reduce one's mental flexibility and even one's intelligence. We must die to ourselves at every moment. But to do so one needs a solar consciousness.

19. You can awaken suddenly from the illusion of the crystallized Dragon, which is so full of solitude and anguish, and then fall in step with the melody of the universal dance by means of which the oneness of sound spreads out in a myriad of rhythm-events.

20. When we contemplate the luminous and questioning beauty of a child's eyes, we receive streams of vibrations to which we may respond or not, depending on the superimpositions we are able to eliminate from the field of our consciousness.

21. A geometrical birch leaf reveals itself through its particular order which depends on a proper vibratory ratio, that is through its specific tonal accord. This can be experienced by our consciousness in the measure in which we are able to eliminate the superimpositions of our mind.

22. When we gaze in ecstasy at a rose bud, at its vibrant and soft harmony of colors, we savor an Accord, a symphony of rhythms, a whirlwind of Beauty.

But if mental superimpositions fall within our field of consciousness, the enchantment is broken, and subject and object emerge in opposition to each other.

23. To realize an Accord among the various individual energetic components (instinct-feeling-thought, etc.) means achieving a new product, a new transfiguring condition; it means finding Harmony, which must be perceived, heard and grasped by our inner life, because only what is experienced inwardly possesses a real value.

24. When we comprehend the number and the tonal value that vibrate in all things we can hear the Harmony that pervades the living whole and whose laws are revealed by the proper Accord. This implies emerging from all conceptual frameworks, from each and every empirical superimposition.

25. The reciprocal vibratory relationship between the colors of a flower, its perfume and its spatial-molecular geometry generates a symphonic Accord that our listening consciousness can experience.

We can *vibrate* in Love-Accord with universal Life because we are a part of this Life. To do so, the mind must be silent, the subconsciousness must not superimpose its past, its judgement and its noise upon all this enchantment. Life cannot be judged or conceptualized; one must simply love it for what it is. When the ego ceases to operate, then Life absorbs us and we are able to comprehend its dimension, Harmony and Beauty.

26. Scientific discoveries have proven that the atom itself, which is fire, vanishes into the without-form. We can experience this formless condition of Fire insofar as we do not superimpose our composite and formal fire upon it.

The non-formal is our goal because *we are* the non-formal itself.

27. The universe of names and forms is a vibrating and resounding energy compound. To live within it does not imply a state of conflict. Conflict emerges when we wish to assign absolute Reality to it. In this case, we mistake «the snake for the rope»[1], the image-picture for the screen. The endless rhythmical forms of light and shadow flicker upon the *screen* of the Infinite producing geometrical flames of events.

Those who grasp the difference between the spectacle and the unqualified Witness have reached the threshold of Realization.

28. These are the characteristics of the Realized:

---

[1] See, Śaṅkara,*Vivekacūḍāmaṇi*, 110. Translation form the Sanskrit and Commentary by Raphael, Aurea Vidyā. New York.

«He possesses nothing, yet he is always satisfied; he has no aid, yet he possesses all power; he does not delight in objects, yet he is always content; he has no equal to him, yet he considers all and everybody with equanimity».

«Although he acts he remains inactive; although he experiences the fruits of past actions he is not touched by them; although he has a body of flesh he does not identify with it; although limited he is omnipresent»[1].

29. Upon the head of the Awakened there burns the sign of Fire.

In the Heart of the Awakened there lives a cross of flame that does not burn.

30. «They are two, hidden within the secret folds of the Infinite: Ignorance and Knowledge»[2]. The Awakened has transcended both of these because they are both superimpositions upon the Supreme Reality.

31. If you live and operate within time, then you cannot obtain a metaphysical vision of Truth.

To emerge from time, you must distil your Demeter with the Vinegar and regenerate Dionysus so that the a-temporal Fire may shine.

---

[1] Śaṅkara, *Vivekacūḍāmaṇi*, 543-544, Op. cit.

[2] *Śvetāśvatāra Upaniṣad*, I, V, 1, in, *Upaniṣad*, Edited by Raphael. Op. cit.

III

PAIN-SUFFERING

1. What is the value of suffering and pain?

They are the symbol of an error, a wrong direction taken by desire-action.

Pain is not error in itself, but it is its consequence and, as symbol, it reveals its precise meaning to the extent it is comprehended.

Suffering serves no purpose if one does not recognize the error which is the cause of suffering.

2. If pain is the result of a wrong direction given to energy, then comprehension of oneself, and thus of things, brings pain to an end.

3. We have knowledge-awareness of a thing and awareness of our *reaction* to that thing.

The first movement is simple observation-contemplation devoid of all possible evaluation or judgement; it is pure vision.

The second movement is the outcome of subconscious coloring by accumulation and memory. Usually we are trapped inside our descriptive, interpretative and emotional reactions and therefore we are outside true knowledge and life. Sooner or later reaction means, conflict and suffering.

4. We should carefully avoid placing pain upon the altar of devotion and adoration; pain, like pleasure, is a simple egoistical qualification. Truth is beyond pain-pleasure. The Self transcends all duality.

5. Humanity seems to have chosen the way of pain in its quest for supreme Truth.
Through its deep conflict and exhausting suffering it will slowly manage to find its Fire of Life, or its resolving Sulphur.

6. In time and space pain may scorch the consciousness, but slowly that arid soil will moisten and be ready to yield good fruits. Likewise, the sun brings drought to the fields but at the right moment it also brings the Water of life. The proper dosage of Fire can resolve the cause of pain.

7. The Realized does not suffer or rejoice when faced with experiences of others, or with his own. The Sage is not saddened by the death of others or by his own. The Libearated does not *react*, but comprehends the flow of events.

8. To break the chains of pain you must make the pure part of the fixed lead volatile with that *solvent* of ours, and fix your spring Water with the power of Fire; in this way you will obtain a spiritualized Body and a solidified, fixed or corporeal Spirit.

9. Between two ideas or two states (waking and dreaming, etc.) there is the Constant. But the empirical ego is used to living in the *discontinuum* of time-space and it is unable

to detach itself from it, because it considers the Constant and Fullness as mere emptiness.

«In the presence of God the wise are mad and the mad are wise»[1].

10. When a desire is not achieved the empirical ego seeks compensations which, in turn, represent a state of duality and therefore of apprehension, pleasure-pain and bewilderment.

We seek happiness because in truth our intimate nature is Bliss, but unfortunately we seek it in objects (sensations, emotions, thoughts, etc.), objects that represent, after all, conflict and confusion.

Sooner or later one must come to the conclusion that true Bliss can only be within oneself, in the most secret corner of our Heart. It reveals itself when all is quiet, when the objects vanish and when the "vessel" has been transfigured.

11. Pain may be the frozen isolation which transfigures one into a furnace of Love.

Pain may be the loss of everything which is followed by the possession of transcendental riches.

Pain is the whip that urges the wanderer to build the structure of his inner Temple in a perfect way.

Those who have overcome pain have overcome all limitations, and this reveals Beauty.

12. Death – even the death of a psychic content – is anguish and pain for the "profane" person but it is joy and liberation for the Sage.

---

[1] Paul, *Letter to the Corinthians*, III, 19.

13. If pain rushes frighteningly toward you, contemplate it, observe it and question it; it may bring you a message of freedom.

14. Suffering is the outcome of the lost Good. Do not allow regret to prevail but apply yourself to the *Opus* and take back what belongs to you. The key that opens the kingdom of Heaven is the Philosophers' Fire.

15. Suffering approaches everybody, good as well as bad, because everybody can err. There is no God who rewards and punishes, there is simply the individual who can direct himself either toward pain or toward the splendor of Beauty.

16. It is beautiful to see a face lined by tears that have watered the roots of radiant Love and the urge to fly like an Eagle.

17. Radiant Love is the law of Harmony and of Accord whereas pain and suffering are the product of physical, psychic or spiritual disharmony. Whoever loves truly is attuned to Life; Eros is the power which unifies, exalts and sublimates.

18. A moment of anguish blocks the entire psycho-physical mechanism thus producing disharmony and isolation; a moment of radiant Love releases energy that beneficially spreads out – like the spokes from the hub of a wheel – as far as the farthest Circumference.

19. Egocentric, sensorial happiness isolates; pain, when it is understood, unifies and comforts. The disciple on the way to Awakening may suffer because he is still egocentric.

20. How much suffering there is for mankind! And yet these sufferings could all be eliminated in a very short time; it would be sufficient to place oneself in a *proper* perspective, thus readjusting all values.

21. The great cosmic spheres are created by the rhythm-harmony that fills the interstellar space.

How can these rhythms be captured?

How can we prepare our vehicle of contact so that we may comprehend these harmonics?

How can we re-educate our consciousness to tune in to the inner sound of Being? The mind produces suffering or pleasure, pain or joy, disharmony or harmony; with our vibrating *string* we can offer a choir of harmonic rhythms or discordant and disturbing notes to ourselves and to others.

22. The vibrating string can resonate at various levels or vibrations of accord. The individual can raise his vibrations higher and higher so as to create accord with the indefinite universal Hierarchies.

The human consciousness can harmonize with a flower, an animal or with another human unity of consciousness, with the Angels or with God. It can attune itself to joy, pain, suffering, anxiety, egoism or Love. It all depends upon the tension of the string, on the way in which that consciousness vibrates, lives and determines itself.

23. It is inevitable that, sooner or later, the human being will become aware of his inner string-consciousness. Present day psychology represents the first attempt at revealing man's energy expressions at the instinctual, emotional, mental and behavioral level.

Slowly the individual must realize that the internal universe is regulated by as many laws as the external, objective world. To comprehend these laws means freeing oneself from the slavery of anxiety, pain, suffering and conflict, just as knowledge of the laws of the external universe frees him from the bondage of need.

24. Comprehend the laws that govern you. Along your spinal *shaft* run two substances, the one burning and fiery, the other watery and cold. It may sometimes happen during the ascesis of the *Opus* that one perceives either the one or the other, which are not of a strictly metallic and vulgar order. If you manage to bring these two substances to the *bottom* of your "hermetic vessel" they will fuse and mix thus preparing the philosophical Mercury of which you have often been told. This Mercury, under the influence of Fire, awakens the Stone, or a third Substance which, shining as one hundred suns, rises, takes flight and transfigures your saturnine vessel into Beauty and radiance. When the Groom and the Bride meet they generate a Child of marvelous Beauty and of magical Power.

25. This Child is called Awakened and expresses vibratory qualities that revive Harmony. In a world of discordant vibrations Harmony and Accord can reveal themselves in the same measure as the individual's expressive qualities manage to tune in with the Accord-Harmony of that Child of Glory.

26. Every *Avatāra* is a powerful rhythm of Light vibrating against the background of the Infinite. Those who have a trained ear can hear that rhythm even after thousands of years. What a pity that the conflicted individual does not pay attention to the beauty of Accord. We implore Harmony, health, joy, etc., without thinking that these qualities are with us, around us... within us.

We seek afar what can be found so close. Let us re-educate our " mechanism of contact" and vibrate with the Music of the spheres.

27. Why not enable this planet of pain to vibrate with joy and harmony? Nothing can prevent us from doing so except our blindness, ignorance and pride. We are commensurate with Beauty only when the thorns of ugliness have been crushed within us.

28. Attractions and repulsions keep us tied to many people and things, thus conditioning us.

Unconsciously or consciously we think, feel and move according to these two vibratory states and very little is left to our freedom of choice.

Attraction-repulsion creates distortions within our vessel, thus altering the Accord and the right note.

To escape from this kind of enslaving duality means listening to the rhythm of life in the proper way, from the right stand-point, with an attentive *Heart*; it means following the "Pathway of Fire".

29. We are more strongly bound to the person we hate than to the one we love. Individual love can, to a certain

extent, be transmuted into universal love, but to transform hatred into fondness and comprehension is indeed difficult.

30. Whoever is able to consider life dispassionately, and through intelligence retrace its causes and effects, will comprehend that attraction and repulsion, in their gross form, are largely responsible for human suffering. Without the fixed Mercury, one is at the mercy of psychological dualism.

31. Every micro and macrocosmic movement is supported by Love. If you place yourself at the center of the universal vortex, you will be radiant Love, like the morning star. Then, conflict and pain will be distant things for you.

IV

THE EMPIRICAL EGO

1. Can we look at things and events without involving the representative ego?

Can we observe a thing in a direct way without the intrusion of the imagining mind?

Can we be pure contemplative fire without thought that describes and compares?

When the empirical ego arises in a relationship, it relies upon memory, comparison, culture, distinction and upon the representation of reality rather than upon reality in itself.

2. The ego-accumulation puts up barriers, creates dualism, opposition and distance. The ego is a mental stratification, a focal reverberation capable of conditioning a being's life.

The death of the phenomenal ego is the death of pain and the wedding of the alchemical Sulphur and Mercury.

3. The ego lives and perpetuates itself by pitying and loving itself.

The ego is not capable of true love and therefore of effective magnetism, because it is too taken up in creating mechanisms of defence and protection. The ego sees only the ego, therefore only itself. Radiant Love demands completeness and unity of consciousness.

Love is the magical agent that permits you to saturate the phases of the *Opus*. Remember that Love moves and unites the substances of the *Opus*, while Will gives concentrated and determined strength, and Intelligence bestows wise direction.

Therefore, it is through the transcendence of the ego that an ascesis may be joyfully accomplished[1].

4.   The ego criticizes and condemns society without realizing that society is simply a sum of egos. Not having the courage to look at its own intrinsic misery, it projects it outward, thus avoiding the basic problem and its resulting solution.

The ego always preaches for others, never for itself.

5. All opposites (such as ego and non-ego) are mutually dependent; therefore a thing is determined by its opposite; it can exist only in a relationship. All data that live of reciprocity are simple modal aspects of a single reality: thought; which means that they are similar. We can say that opposites contain each other; therefore, to move toward any opposite does not mean to emerge from the relational framework. From this we can deduce that stepping into the corridor of opposites leads to pain.

If we wish to emerge from the conditioning of polarities we must remain in the *point at the center*, and that means resolving and transcending *change*, which is becoming.

---

[1] For the further study for an ascesis see, Raphael, *Beyond the illusion of the ego*, Synthesis of a Realizative Process, Aurea Vidyā, New York.

6. When we say that we wish to transform ourselves we must realize that it is always the ego that is *desiring* and projecting. Our true transformation occurs when, ceasing to wish for our transformation, we remain steadfast in the mental non-motion, in timelessness, beyond all desiring and causing.

7. What people call intelligence is really simple ability, virtuosity and dexterity shown by the empirical ego in connection with some expressive human activity.

Sometimes intelligence is bartered with demagogic cunning and egoistical guile. True intelligence is that which let us open the door toward the intelligible, toward the supreme Good.

8. There is an action inherent in the empirical ego which, sooner or later, produces pain-conflict but there is also an action which springs from mental silence, which is the truest, most positive and harmonic action. When we have transcended the world of contradictory thought and therefore of ego, we have also transcended the enslaving action. We must reveal *action without action*, and this is characteristic of a consciousness that has grasped the workings of the mind and cleansed our Magnesia.

9. The ego drowns in time and time falls upon the grieving consciousness bringing with it tear drops and disequilibrium.

Consecrate yourself to the extraction of that Mercury of ours; Mercury is the harbinger of the non-reflected Light sweeping through timelessness.

10. By desiring the ego creates a distance between itself and the desired event. This distance is expectation, becoming, effort, conflict and pain.

With the death of the ego the being discovers itself to be bliss without object, without distance or time.

11. One must distinguish between Being and being this or that, between the "I am what I am" and the "I am this or that", between discovering oneself without name and form and living for names and forms; only a profound act of discernment can help us to recognize the essential nature of our true being.

12. Many confuse self-realization with self-assertion or assertion of the ego as individuality. They believe that self-realization means taking care of the ego, thinking of the ego, indoctrinating the ego and looking after themselves as *individuals*. Some are in good faith, others alas, are not.

Self-realization means to reveal the Essence-Principle and Fullness that are *beyond the ego* and all its attributes. Realization of oneself means knowledge of oneself, and to truly know oneself means the end of conflict, bewilderment and all kinds of appropriation; it is the most beautiful gift that one can offer Life, the most profitable service one can render to others.

13. The ego divides and fragments Unity. Self-realization brings Unity back to its proper place. All things resolve themselves into Unity and Unity is the goal of all things, the aim of the "Pathway of Fire". There is no greater awareness than that of unifying Salt, Mercury and Sulphur in the incommensurable One-without-a-second.

14. It is well to insist upon the distinction between the ego amalgamated with the lower quaternary and the Self or ontological I, which represents the universal Consciousness in us: *Puruṣa, ātman*, Being, *Noûs*.

The psychological ego is always inflated. During the day we appear with different egos or *senses* of the ego. Our social ego is not the same as that used in the office, just as the ego we present in the office is not the one we show at home, as our home ego is not the one with which we meet our friends, etc. The ego is a chameleon which changes its aspect according to the circumstances. To believe in the ego's masks is senseless. Much suffering could be avoided if one took this indoctrinated chamaeleon less seriously.

Our deeper and supreme I, or Self, represents the metaphysical foundation of the empirical, contingent ego. And we, as ultimate and constant reality, are the imperishable immortal Self, beyond birth and death. All true initiatory processes lead to the realization of this supreme I and to the death of that ego, which, after all, *is not*.

15. Living means acting. But when this acting is the cause of bewilderment and conflict, can we ever say that we really live?

To really live, and therefore to live harmoniously, we must know how to act. But can we find an action devoid of vanity, distinction, oppression, compensation, competition, greed and other limitations of that kind?

There is an art of living which requires *supreme realization*. The true being is one who, at all times, plays the note of Beauty upon the harp of space.

16. Humans' thoughts are divided into *mine* and *yours*. There is even mention of *my* God and *your* God. This division into mine and yours is the cause of all evil. When mine and yours dissolve into *ours*, we can arrive at the time of universal fruition and Accord.

17. The "sense of ego" consists in relating every experience to oneself as a separate and opposing entity. But no experience, however beautiful, can ever give true fulfilment to the "sense of ego".

The ego is the sum of unsatisfied desires. True fulfilment cannot be found upon the plane of desire but in the death of desire itself, therefore, in the death of the psychical ego. There is a fleeting ego that experiences within the plane of becoming and there is a Fire-Life which reveals itself in its unconditioned state and impersonality. The former is accumulated ignorance while the latter, which emerges from the death of the other, is the true being which is.

18. Only with the Mercury of the Philosophers can one discover life without a greedy and conflicting ego. The condition of consciousness is that of being in the world but not of the world. Freed from the ego, one is liberated from all the attributes inherent in the ego, which means being truly at peace with oneself and therefore with the whole of Life.

19. All *reaction* is the fruit of a frustrated ego, whose eagerness and weakness have not been gratified. All reaction is ignorance, which must be eliminated and resolved.

20. One who is without reaction lives in the free flow of life, upon the plane of non-resistance and enjoys great liberty. One who has overcome every reaction has transcended all opposition, contraposition, and has resolved the "mine" and the "yours". So, kill your vulgar Mercury and let the incorruptible Fire triumph.

21. The mind projects the subject and the object (ego and non-ego). Then the subject wants to know the object as if it were a distinct thing.

In this chase to capture the moving object, the subject does not realize that the object is nothing but the other face of itself. It is as if the thief dresses up as a policeman to capture the thief that is again himself. Opposites are identical because their matrix is identical. Discursive, representative or empirical knowledge is becoming, process and ignorance.

22. There are doctrines that rest upon evolution without realizing that evolution means time and time is simply an invention of the ego which strives to perpetuate its condensed Salt.

23. The ego is a mental image, not a reality in itself; and by identifying with it, consciousness defends, protects and nourishes it.

We are constantly being impelled, constrained and enslaved by the *images* produced by the lunar Mercury. We are imprisoned in the web that we built for ourselves through the power of our mental fire. To comprehend the process of imprisonment means being free.

24. We want to be this or that, to pursue ideals and make our dreams come true and so on. But who is it that wants to be this or that and all the rest?

That is someone or something that, in fact, *is not*. As if it were, it would not desire anything. Now the ego, which is not, deludedly believes to be *becoming*, therefore it moves and experiences by transmigrating, forced by its own incompleteness.

The Self, or the ontological I, does not move, experience or desire, because it *is*.

The Complete one rests upon his very own completeness.

25. We are at war one against the other because we are at war with ourselves. We shall never be able to establish Order, Accord, Harmony – attributes of the Philosophers' Gold – until that time when Harmony is conquered by the consciousness of the individuals.

Those who assert that Order can be established without being first realized by the individuals, are far from comprehending the cause that determines human conflict.

26. The phenomenal ego is a reference point within becoming. The individual, having always related experiences to a *me*, has fostered the crystallization of a separate and relative entity called *ego*. This ego is adherence to the fleeting things, events, bodies, etc., of the moment. The "I am this" of today is not the "I am this" of yesterday. What gives continuity to the ego consciousness is memory, and memory is subconsciousness and imprisoning condensation.

27. The ego mistakes its own selfishness and desire for love, and this form-image in the consciousness is such that when one speaks of love one cannot but relate it to a need felt by one's own or other people's egos.

For the world of ego, to please the desires of an individual, means to love that individual. The being's greatest weakness toward others is considered to be love. For thousands of years humanity has spoken of love, but Love still has to be discovered and revealed. When that will be done, society will live in perfect Accord and in true participation of hearts.

28. Love is accord with the essence of life. When a being lives in Unity one will comprehend that every atom of life is nothing but a part of oneself.

This recognition shatters the greedy and selfish ego and reveals the harmony of Beauty.

29. The ego seeks comfort and not a solution, commiseration and not a dialogue, erudition and not knowledge, love of itself and not comprehension, it seeks ideals by which to perpetuate itself and not Silence, which is wisdom and completeness. The "Pathway of Fire" implies the death of the phenomenal ego and the awakening of the interred Body of glory.

30. Condensed Fire is also composed of saṁsāric ego, of the phantom that haunts us with all its desire and hunger for earthly experiences. The empirical ego is awareness of time. The ego of today has a face and a name that do not coincide with those of the ego of a distant past.

The individualized spark of Fire interprets, upon the great screen of the world's stage, now one ego-character and now another ego.

The ego-character is a reflection of the manifest Spark (Soul) and this, in turn, is the reflection of colorless Fire (Self).

If we enter into the consciousness of the Soul upon its own plane, we can remember some of the ego-characters that we interpreted as time went by. But this is of no importance: to become aware of one's past illusions does not help one to solve one's existential problems. Illusion only creates illusion just as time only leads to time.

31. In its higher aspect, the "Pathway of Fire" reveals the art of *dying*, of discovering oneself as *skeleton*.

True Life is born not of profane death but of the *Ars moriendi*, which is the death of the Philosophers. In order to be dazzling Sun one must first undergo "putrefaction" and "trituration".

V

MEDITATION

1. We can divide the various kinds of meditation into two groups: meditation with an object or seed and meditation without an object. Meditation with a seed is the easier of the two and is more accessible to the aspirant. It consists in focusing on an object of meditation-contemplation, be it concrete or abstract: it might be Christ, Kṛṣṇa, Buddha, one's Self (as an object), love, goodness, etc.

The meditator concentrates on these images with increasing intensity until he fuses with them. In this way he arrives at a state of unity.

Meditation without an object is the direct way and is meant for those who have exceptional powers of abstraction and of intuition. It is a method of elimination, reduction and regression that requires the supervision of a Knower.

Through this type of meditation one discovers the ultimate nature of the object, thus achieving the non-formal.

2. The most direct route is not necessarily the quickest; in fact it is very difficult. It requires an uncommon kind of Comprehension, because the mind finds it very hard to abandon its discursive perceptive schemes.

3. The direct route takes us to the elimination of subject-object, experiencer and experienced. We thus reach a great Silence, which is neither the void nor nothingness but profound Fullness and non-dual Presence.

4. True meditation is that which transcends thought. It is meditation without mental activity. Silence is an eternal language that can be heard and comprehended. Silence is mute eloquence, revelation of the Real and the Principle of Fire.

5. Between in-breath and out-breath, between death and rebirth, between one *manvantara* and another there is a void – suspension of every film-event – in which the screen of the Infinite reveals itself in all its clarity and greatness.

6. Every true work of art is an object that tends to eliminate itself as a mere object, thus leaving the way open to the underlying Reality.

Every seed of meditation must allow the Substratum, the Constant to emerge.

7. If the vertical and horizontal components in a work of architecture are perfectly balanced and top and bottom offset each other, then the object-creation loses all its objective importance thus revealing its intimate and hidden harmony, its non-formal dimension.

In the spatiality of the human psyche, when non-desire balances the entire energy compound, the non-formal reveals itself in all its harmonious majesty.

8. The supreme Self, the ontological I, the Witness without birth or death remains eternally present notwithstanding the countless changes of forms. It is in relation with the empirical ego and its projections that the Self seems to dim and cease to be.

Thus, cinema images seems to exist in their own right, but that is simply an illusion. They can emerge only if there is a screen upon which they are reflected. With meditation we should actualize the elimination of all the changing and finite superimpositions that appear on the screen and reach the fullness of that which is always identical with itself and is the origin of all.

Projection-images (body, emotions, thoughts and the endless gross and subtle forms) are born, grow and die: they constitute becoming. The screen-Self remains in its absoluteness because it is *causa sui*.

Meditation must not be a process of accumulation, but one of elimination and of detachment from time-space-cause. In this way the Constant in us reveals itself spontaneously and innocently.

9. We can have this resolving meditative sequence:

– Elimination of the object (the various images on the screen. Becoming).

– Elimination of the subject (the experiencer of the images. The acting empirical ego).

– Identity with the screen-Self (Fullness).

10. How can we grasp the Real? The Real is that which is and does not become and is self-revealing, not depending

on anything outside of itself. While being the metaphysical basis of that which becomes, it is outside of it, and while being the cause-producing factor, it is uncaused.

If the Real were becoming we could not have stable knowledge nor any exact science; everything would turn out to be not only uncertain and precarious but accidental conception, vision and action.

The individual would be forever involved in non-substantial movement. If all were becoming, including human beings, where would they find the concepts of constancy, of immortality and of without-time-space?

11. Silence is the most powerful form of communication. If a simple sound produced by the vocal chords is quite strong, then what will the "silent ultrasound" produced by the Realized at certain levels of being, be like?

12. True glory consists in ceasing... to exist. To reveal this state a total and complete sacrifice is required.

In such a condition we can slowly and with growing persistence feel a transcendent Power pushing us toward the central Fire that is within us. This is the beginning of total abstraction and resolution.

13. The most resolving form of meditation is Comprehension. It is the direct pathway that leads to the heart of Being.

To Comprehend is to have truth with oneself. Those who Comprehend create identity with Reality.

14. To comprehend means to completely strip oneself of all subconscious contents and of all the crystallizations of the collective unconscious.

Comprehension implies deep attention, a calm and stable mind and a perceptive intensity without opposition.

15. To comprehend means to permeate the entire consciousness with revealed truth: this involves catharsis. True Comprehension is not of a sensorial order. To grasp a thing intellectually is one thing, to *comprehend it* is another.

In comprehension there is the active work of consciousness, there is ascensional fire, there is synthesis and mastery of the "inner hearing".

16. In every condition of consciousness, analysis distinguishes the witness-substratum from the subject and the object of knowledge.

Consciousness transcends these two. We are aware of our individuality, therefore we can transcend it.

It is because we do not make this distinction that false superimpositions fix themselves upon our consciousness-witness. In order to be able to detach ourselves from an object we must know how to place ourselves at the proper focal distance. When we comprehend the nature of the subject and the object it is not we who detach ourselves, it is they that fade away until they vanish completely.

17. Identity with the ontological I is outside of every physical and mental framework. Our true nature transcends all that. To grasp this truth and be convinced of the validity

of the transcendence of the empirical consciousness, we must *ask questions of ourselves.*

It is easy to sit at the feet of someone with a passive and inert mind but it is difficult to question oneself. This requires great humility, detachment and an inquiring spirit. The initiatory path is one of self-realization.

18. There is another form of meditation that is immensely beneficial: *dialogue.* In a true dialogue there is no competition or vanity, no past and no empirical ego.

In dialogue there is simply research, unveiling of Reality, "tension without effort" and creation of a magnetic field which favours osmosis and interaction of ideas. Dialogue is also made up of silences, waiting and pauses. Dialogue between two hearts is Love.

19. In deep meditation the consumption of oxygen and the elimination of carbon dioxide diminish. A reduction in the speed of metabolism (and therefore in the need for oxygen) corresponds with a practically involuntary decrease of the speed of breathing and therefore of the quantity of air inhaled. Besides, there is also a diminution of hematic lactate produced by the anaerobic metabolism. Normally the concentration of lactate in the body diminishes in a resting subject.

There is also an increase in the intensity of the slow "alpha" waves in the brain.

All this, and many other things besides, can bring great benefit to the physical compound, apart from the strictly spiritual results. Meditation places the psycho-physical being in an optimum state of energetic interrelations and electromagnetic and glandular harmonization.

20. The ego does not exist if not to create identification with an object of knowledge, and persistent identification is a habit and accumulation that hinders Realization enormously.

One may identify with the emotion of sex, hatred, anxiety, etc., but all these emotions are nothing but objects of knowledge which belong to the world of duality and becoming. In mental silence all duality disappears. Meditation must gradually lead us to the essence of Fire. Insofar as one fixes the Mercury of the Philosophers the powers of the black Dragon subside.

21. The body, the mind and all that makes up our individuality are continually changing. *One* who observes and perceives this entire process cannot be touched by it, otherwise how could he observe and perceive it?

This "One" is therefore corporeal Mercury, the *Consciousness-witness* of thought emotion and action in the state of waking, dreaming and deep sleep. Beyond the becoming-process, or individualized formal fire, there is "That" which is always identical to itself and distinct from time-space-cause and from ego and non-ego.

22. The fire of meditation burns every remnant in the psycho-physical spatiality and accords and harmonizes the mind with the Infinite.

When we fall into deep meditation before the beauty of a rose our consciousness-mind can tune itself in with the archetypal divine beauty and taste the rainbows of eternity.

23. Our Hermetic Sun is hidden by an opaque, slimy and black disc. By means of the secret Agent, the Philosopher's faithful and loyal servant, is moistened and raised to the Zenith

so that the shadows are dispelled and scattered. Only thus can the conflicting ego be completely shattered.

24. How can the individual ego be the ultimate Reality? Less cannot be more, the part cannot be the Whole and change cannot be the Immutable. Therefore the empirical ego can neither be the consciousness-witness nor awareness of "I am what *is*".

25. One must really be awakened to comprehend how difficult it is to make others accept Liberation.

Many approach the sacred Truths in search of sensations, compensation, unusual experiences, further accumulation or mystery.

In order to transcend oneself, it is not enough to be good and moral to serve, nor to make converts. Something else is needed, and that is: to *Be*, and when one *Is*, Space responds adequately.

26. You must comprehend that there are no objects-events without sensitivity, no sensitivity without consciousness, no subjects without objects and no objects without subjects.

The moment we do something, *we* are that thing; only later do we become aware of having acted, therefore the acting subject becomes the object of knowledge or of consciousness. At the moment of *action* we are *one* with it.

Thus, we are so blinded by our interest in the object-event that we assume its identity. If we think appropriately we see that data-events with which we have identified have no independent reality in that they have been perceived. Moreover, they appear and disappear continuously.

Do you perhaps believe that the data-events of dreams have any reality of their own, independently of the dreamer? As they are simply objects of perception, they vanish when the mind ceases its projective-perceptive movement. This condition is identical to that of the waking state.

27. To find oneself in the state of suspension of thought means being free of desires and therefore of accumulation and of memory.

All this opens the door to the experience-non-experience of the Self, the Witness without name and form, without differentiation and without parts. Silence is the power of fullness.

28. In reality we should not use the word "experience" when we refer to identity with the Self. Experience concerns relations between subject and object.

But if we grasp the fact that the supreme Experience is not to be placed within the category of objects, then we also comprehend that all the work of meditation should not aim at perceiving experiences because this would simply lead to a strengthening of that very duality which we must transcend.

The realization of the Self must take place by predisposing the mind toward a correct "inner listening". When all objects disappear from the field of consciousness, then the event takes place, duality disappears and the nature of the Self reveals itself.

29. Meditation with Ardor is the means by which the various fires are coordinated and integrated into one sole Fire, so that consciousness may achieve the flight of the Eagle.

30. The "Pathway of Fire" does not study psychology but it *makes* psychology. Therefore, a *seeking* attitude and pioneering approach is required of those who wish to learn the Art. The sulphureous Fire can reveal itself to an inquiring, humble and loving mind.

Similarly, the "Pathway of Fire" does not study philosophy, but it *makes* philosophy, which implies having a philosophical mind. Since all this must be *lived* and not theorized or schematized, one must possess the rarest of qualifications: that of *wanting to be*.

31. «The brain is the symbol of water and the heart that of Fire»[1].

The brain is a power of the central Fire. The profound intelligence resides in the heart of Fire, an intelligence which links you to the universal and which knows no barriers or needs.

---

[1] *Zohar*: III, 233b.

VI

REALIZATION

1. We observe a rose with all its petals and color and we classify it according to certain botanical schemes, but its ultimate reality escapes us. To know a rose in itself we must know *ourselves* because our Essence is identical to that of the flower.

When we discover our Essence we shall come into contact with the Essence of all things. Existence has but a sole Essence and indefinite varieties of structures-forms.

2. As long as we think that joy could be found in external object-events, our hopes – out of *despair* – will be placed in future object-events, in expectation; in other words, in becoming.

We are suspended in the illusion of the future or else we are immersed or distressed by the memory of the past, never living the Present. The suspension of the imagination-projection movement reveals the Infinite, the point without dimensions.

For those who express this state of without-movement, there is neither past nor future, there is only without-time.

3. Every now and then I return to the *Opus*. Remember that the Humid and the Dry belong to the same nature and that there is a moment when one turns into the other.

Chokmah and *Binah*, in the Sephirothic Tree (of the *Qabbālāh*), are the children of the same Father. Dryness and Humidity are brother and sister and during a certain phase of the *Opus* they must create an incest.

4. Time is the measure of movement-process-evolution, therefore to speak of motion is tantamount to speaking of time. The timeless or eternally present or constitutes an integral completeness, that which *is* in all its indivisible reality.

Thought is time-process-movement, therefore in the ceasing of thought, time vanishes and being savors a-temporality, that is, itself in its unconditioned state.

5. Integral Liberation is not achieved by merely observing fasting or particular rituals, but by means of Knowledge (Gnosis), which alone can resolve causality, time and space, excluding thus relapses into ignorance-unknowing.

6. Between one perception and another, between one idea and another, between a quantum of light and another there is the "continuum", the suspension, the void, that is to say the Infinite. Happy is the person who knows how to capture and live this "continuum" of Fullness.

7. The void frightens us because it is the negation of that which we call corporeal-sensorial existence.

Until we emerge from the formal concept-framework, the non-formal appears to us as emptiness, and in order not to enter into it we try and objectify thought-forms, that is to say illusions.

Thus we lose a stupendous chance of discovering that we are true Being.

8. Fear, doubt, pessimism and anguish preclude the revelation of the non-formal. They constitute the stratifications which we ourselves have constructed in time-space.

9. For the individual who is in complete harmony with himself and the cosmos, breathing takes on a deep metaphysical significance. It is the symbol of an accord, of a rhythm existing between oneself and the Principle. Each in-breath expresses a rising up toward cosmic Harmony, each out-breath means spreading the accord in the manifest dimension; each retention of breath means complete abandon to the Principle.

10. According to *Vedānta* metaphysics, unstable and tumultuous emotion, belongs to the strength of *rajas*, while serenity and peace belong to the condition of *sattva*. It is the *sattva* possibility that favours authentic discernment between Real and non-real.

One who remains impersonal, beyond egotism, has completely transcended the sphere of emotion, therefore he finds himself in a state of freedom, in no way conditioned by personal requests and ready to reveal the ultimate Reality, which is fullness.

11. Humility is a characteristic of pure intellect and in order to *comprehend*, great humility is needed. It determines living a present situation as it is and not as one believes it should be. The humble person neither lowers nor exalts himself, but grasps his true position within the scheme of things.

12. There are three fundamental experiences of oneness:

a) Identity with the object-form-spectacle (the Alchemical Dragon).

b) Identity with the experiencer-subject (Rectified Mercury).

c) Identity with the substratum of the two, which is the absolute screen, the Self, the One-without-a-second (the ultimate and supreme Sulphur).

13. There are many partial truths and one absolute Reality. This is not a temporal-spatial perception-experience. To capture it one requires great Silence, humility and an urge toward the non-formal.

14. During the passage of the consciousness from the formal to the non-formal there comes an obscurity derived from the state of confusion and vagueness of the elements. But if the consciousness penetrates more deeply it sees the *virgin light* of the Spirit by which it can make all things new again.

15. The various bodies of being are nothing but crystallized form-images produced by the mental fire.

That which the mental fire has created, that very fire can dissolve and resolve; so one can pass from the formal to the non-formal, or from the sensible to the intelligible.

16. Reality must not be mistaken for any particular belief because it remains available and receptive in all its innocent essentiality. In It there is only one evidence, that of pure Existence.

17. One who aims at the ultimate Reality is not preoccupied with the things of the world because these appear to be fleeting and senseless to him. He is interested, rather, in the Constant, where all things, like a rainbow with all of its colors, appear and disappear.

18. How can *One* who was never born, is always identical to himself and will never die, speak of birth and death, of slavery or liberation? If one has the strength and the urge to recognize and establish oneself in the *One who is*, then one can at once transcend the world of appearances.

19. Common beings love mystery, not the Philosophers' Fire. They love activism which they deem useful and good, not the Silence that molds and creates Identity; they merely seek behavioral suggestions, not a resolving Doctrine.

20. In the common person, thought is used to serve subconscious desire. In the Awakened all thought is adequate to the circumstances.

In the former, the mind projects endless images-ideas that leave a trace destined to swell the subconscious more and more. In the latter, every idea-image is born and dies in an instant without leaving any trace or subconscious force-content. This also implies being free from the process of cause-effect.

21. The mind as an instrument of cognition will be useful until we realize the Self, which shines of its own light. To find our way at night we need reflected light such as that of the moon, but when the great solar Fire rises of what use can that pale reflection be?

22. Rather than observe the genuflections, passive devotion, emotional activism or exaltation of his disciple, the Sage philosopher tries to find out to what extent the separating ego and the obscuring veil of illusion have vanished from him.

23. The initiatory Tradition does not represent an accumulation of cognitions aimed at instructing and teaching some secret, but it reveals to those who are ready for it a movement capable of revolutionizing the consciousness and it lights a Fire that purifies, renews and transfigures.

24. The *form* that we observe and which we call tree is not in the tree but it exists in our mind, which assumes the form-image of whatever object it perceives; the consciousness identifies with it and is trapped. If the mind is educated so as not to take form, it remains calm, homogeneous and undifferentiated and the very notion of the ego-conflict disappears. It is like the sea without waves, ripples, or movement; it remains attentive, receptive, free of accumulation and of subconscious contents, beyond all pain-pleasure.

This mind, emptied of becoming-bondage, is at last ready for the final step of realization. It must simply wait for the great Silence to blossom, without forcing or desiring it (this would only mean creating further conflicting wave-forms and consequent identification), it must simply wait for it because it will certainly come – for this is the inevitable law of Being.

25. So much energy is employed in desiring! What extraordinary force a being is capable of producing to take possession of an object... which is fleeting. If this same energy were used to realize the Self, It would reveal itself in a flash. But the individual, in all his wilful blindness, continues to

acquire conflict and pain instead of Bliss. We have placed pain and suffering upon the altar, deified anguish and distress and built up the cult of the ego, which is illusion and bewilderment.

26. Realization is sacred Lætizia (Joy), Serenity permeated by Love and divine detachment; it is incommensurable placidity which cadences space according to perfect geometries of accord, and thus in Harmony with the whole of manifest and non-manifest life.

27. When we observe a mineral, a vegetable, an animal, a star, a planet, a lovely face or a beautiful flower, when we contemplate a smile or the gaze of a child we find ourselves in front of a harmony of chords and rhythms. Whoever grasps this reality – without conditioning or subconscious colorings – vibrates with the universe, with life and with the Love of the Philosophers.

28. What does seeing an object mean? It means that our eyes respond to the vibrations of light emanated by the object; let us remain in this communion of accord and rhythm, in this osmosis of life. When the mind wants to transform this harmony of bliss into nominal and formal concepts, when it wants to crystallize the flow of life, the enchantment is broken. Then the mind, unable to remain Silent and taste the Eternal, produces only a weak and feeble conceptualized reflection of the throbbing and living reality.

29. To acquire information, by means of a book of physics, about the undulatory structure of matter is one thing, to

experience it without any crystallized conceptualization of the ego is quite a different thing.

To get to know the molecular-luminous structure of the universe is one thing, to consciously experience the rhythm of the Harmony of the "quantum" of universal light is something else.

The consciousness-Witness grasps at once the nudity, noumenality and unity of the various "models of light". In this kind of self-awareness one does not see objects that are known to the senses; one has the certainty that all sensations, perceptions, movements, even those of a psychic nature, are based upon undulatory vibrations. One recognizes with evident clarity that the old tridimensional world, which possessed a certain solidity, is nothing but a play of wave-rhythms, which superimpose themselves upon the stuff of the Infinite.

The compound universe crumbles into vibratory waves: mine, yours, his, hers dissolve and the living consciousness throbs with the universal rhythm of Being.

30. Because the nature of the Self permeates our very consciousness, it would seem that one does not need a Master.

Realization is not achieved by means of appropriation; It *is*. But from a practical point of view we can say that the presence of a Master is necessary.

31. If you are travelling and you decide to stop, then all you must do is to stop.

The universe of names and forms is a continuum-discontinuum which can be interrupted at any given moment. Know that all the substances and the means required for the *Opus* live in you and are you.

VII

ROSE GARDEN

1. When we observe an object, a contact is established between it and us; this is the point of departure for conceptual elaboration.

Thus we do not encounter the object itself but our mental construction of it. In other words, we superimpose our own personal ideation upon the object.

Therefore what we call an object is the outcome and product of our imagination. The universe is not the sensorial-imaginative one that we have built for ourselves. When the mind does not imagine but actually *sees* the universe in its intrinsic truth, then the Fire of Knowledge emerges innocently and clearly.

2. Do not think that our past can be resolved in one day by means of simple curiosity or by means of our professional pride. Much more is required. Life stems from "death" and the majority flee "death" because they are afraid of it. But the philosophical Fire reveals itself only to those who burn to ashes the fleeting fires of opinion.

3. The true driving force of the Art is Fire. The influence of Fire makes the virgin substance successively airy,

fiery, liquid and solid, and as a result it may also bring it back to the liquid, fiery, airy and ākāśic state again.

The great rhythms of the substance are kept in the secret of Fire. The power of Fire makes the alchemical matter dance.

4. At the cinema the spectator *enters* into the show. At the end he performs the opposite action, that is, he abandons the show-object and the role of spectator. It is only thanks to this return into oneself that the consciousness without objects is revealed.

The individual *enters* into and identifies with the world of names and forms, the cosmic motion-events involve him and duality overwhelms him. One day he will emerge from this identification with the cosmic-spectacle and will recover his condition of One-without-a-second.

5. Realization is not subject to conditions of time and space. It is not by fleeing to India, Egypt, Tibet, to the North or the South that we can find it. It is inside of ourselves.

Time has no influence over the revelation of our true nature. At any moment we may discover ourselves as Constant or as philosophical Sulphur.

6. The human being does not seek Reality but his own emotional security and, when he does not find it, he creates compensations.

The mind is always chasing after objects, creating duality and strife. It remains the constant prisoner of its own dreams and generates fogginess and aberration. It leads to bondage but it can also lead to liberation.

7. The mind that has not posed the problem of the "why" of things is ignorant and inertial. It is always secreting

thoughts that demand only satisfaction. In other words, it is the prisoner of the alchemical Dragon.

The mind that interrogates itself about the why of things has started its adventure in *seeking*. In this state of tension it may find itself in conflict, in a condition of duality, of suffering and even, at times, of alienation. In its desperate quest it splits, dismembers and disaggregates itself.

With time – which might be thousands of years – the clouds clear away, the light finds its way and the truth begins to emerge. Then, in a flash of resolving intuition, it discovers that... there are no reasons why, and that to ask the reason why is typical of a mind that has not comprehended its own very movement.

When one reaches this peak of awakened tension, the mind no longer produces thought, it has transcended its very own conditioning and in that silence, Being reveals itself in its beingness.

8. Why ask if the ego exists? After all it is always the ego which asks and answers itself. It is the snake biting its own tail. In true living and being, no problem can be born, there can be no questions, no answers, no things to experience, because the postulating ego-experiencer has vanished.

9. No-one can prevent you from being free and yet you force yourself to live in bondage and in limitation. In all your sentimental weakness you prefer to imagine that there is someone, inside or outside of you, hindering your freedom, but remember that this someone is yourself.

10. Every form-object is composed of five elements: Being, Consciousness, Fullness, name and form. When we

eliminate name and form, we are left with the triple unity which shines of its own incorruptible Fire.

11. Only acceptance leads to comprehension and only comprehension produces liberation. Whoever does not accept himself, betrays himself. To overcome ignorance it is necessary, first of all, to recognize it. If you refuse to recognize the Dragon that has you in its grip, then you can never fight it.

12. After having turned *darkness* into radiant *light*, bring yourself to the inner and undivided Center of your being where you will find the *essence* of your form and of all forms, of every dimension and level. In other words, you will find the Philosophers' Stone.

13. The entire past is contained in sounds and visions; it may be decomposed and reconstructed, but the Accomplished has totally transcended it.

A thought is substance of Fire shaped in geometrical forms which remains upon the screen of the Being-Principle until the dream-universe is resolved.

14. The ego of dreams, which lives in incompleteness, cannot escape its past-substance; this follows the thinker just as the shadow follows the body. It is by means of the extraction of the Gold from the cavern that the past vanishes like mist in the sun.

15. The human being's physical body is metallized, though pliable and transformable, fire-energy. All illness can be eliminated by the power of shining Mercury.

16. Why do you seek glory, applause, consensus and the love of others? Why do you seek emotional security and distinction? Why do you condemn yourself to begging a smile, friendship, sex or somebody's acceptance, when there is a condition of Being like that of the sun that lives of its own light? Why do you give in to vulgar products when the purest Gold shines in the depths of your own cavern?

17. The Accomplished does not make converts but simply reveals himself. The Realized does not pass judgement because he finds that everything is in its own right place. The Liberated does not seek to convince because he knows that all opinions in time-space may be valid.

One who *is*, speaks little and only when necessary, because he knows that words serve only to cover up rather than to reveal the Philosophers' Gold.

The Awakened lives in silence because he has placed himself, as consciousness, in the interval between two ideas, therefore in the without-time-space.

The Philosopher of our Art, who has comprehended the end right from the beginning, knows that every event-image returns to the Source. The Philosopher is at the pivot of the scales where he can contemplate all the pairs of duality or of opposites that come and go.

The Liberated look at the primitive, the genius, the saint and the brute with the same equanimous eye.

The Accomplisheds do not seek or compare, they do not desire or refuse, they do not contradict or state, but comprehend and rejoice.

18. Why be preoccupied with the past? It is but emptiness. Why worry about the future? It is a simple mental

projection. Let us kill the enslaving Dragon and let us remain in the timelessness.

19. The presence of doubt, fear and suspicion destroys *contact*, doubt belongs to a mind unable to comprehend.

Attention without tension is Mercurial Fire and this opens up all doors.

20. There is only one Temple and many altars. We battle over the altars, and yet we all belong to the same Temple.

21. A new star appears, grows and explodes. From the non-formal Fire it came and to the non-formal Fire it returns.

Let us proclaim the non-formal Fire, let us pronounce the Name and our bastion will collapse leaving us in total liberty.

22. For the non-formal Fire, the world of names and forms is obscurity, for the universe of names and forms, non formal Fire is emptiness.

23. Can we proclaim the non-formal when for so long we have affirmed only the formal?

We are so used to the shadows that we refuse the light of Fire that cannot be seen by the sensorial eye.

One needs Courage, Daring and Silence. But the conflicting ego is cowardly and backs down when its favorite supports are removed. We have projected insecurity, restlessness and cowardice and now we are their prisoners. The bars of the prison, however, can be broken by daring Philosophers.

24. Are we capable of refusing all the known? Are we capable of abandoning all that does not belong to us? Are we capable of transcending every last scientific, religious and moral truth? When one crosses over the *abyss*, one is always *alone*.

Let us leave others to their petty egos; they are not yet ready to throw the *spear*. Let us close our eyes and resound the Word of Being. The Heavens only point out the way to the strong. It has always been so.

25. Do you think of being born and dying? Do you incline toward death? Do you live in apathy awaiting your "departure" as the balm to heal your sufferings? I must tell you that however much you yearn for it and hope for it, you will never die.

The greatest hoax that life can play on you – oh you who venerate the God of death – is that of making you eternal, and placing you in timelessness.

In the world of Reality there is no place for coming and going, for birth and death.

26. A consciousness that rebels breaks apart the bars of the prison. Let us sharpen the *arrows* of Fire and strike the ignorance that restrains us. Let us proclaim our Dignity which awaits us from time immemorial.

27. The flame of burning Will is quenched in us; we must light the sacred Fire which dwells at the base of our Tower. Once it is lit, the flames of liberation and completeness will burst forth. When the Tower is surrounded by the sacred Fire, a new dawn will appear upon the horizon of life.

Let us proclaim the dawn of Completeness, Beauty and liberating Fire.

28. Every day miracles take place within us, but the eye does not see them. Let us open our *Eye* and we will be amazed to see what lives within our Tower.

29. Times are ripe for triumph. Catastrophe does not frighten us. We must take advantage of this. The Fire is raging all around. Some may be burnt, but others may be transformed, others still may burn ignorance and bondage to ashes.

30. The old proves to be the newest.

What the being tries to pass on as new is simply the repetition of the past, his subconscious crystallization. What is really new is what has always existed and will always exist: it is the eternal present.

True and authentic novelty dwells in the Principle, to the eyes of the individualized soul the Principle is something new, although it really precedes all things. If we want to give form to such a Principle we must identify it with the primordial Tradition which, because it is ageless, is always new.

31. Are we ready for battle? Do we see the square Tower? Do we have the *shield* raised and Fire as our sharp *arrow*? Then let us bring the shield forward and shoot the arrow.

The black needs not be feared, let the white be overtaken and the red be embraced.

VIII

DARING

1. You fear the "death" of the Philosophers because you have not yet comprehended the monstrosity of the scaly Dragon. The day you dare to rend the veil of your phantom bearer of miseries, you will draw the sword of resolving daring and seek that Fire which dissolves the vile imprisoning metal.

2. I give you the key to open the doors of the Temple: there you will find the regenerating Fire which will make you as great as creation, the flaming sword to fight the darkness that restrains you, and the resplendent and constant supreme Truth.

3. Rise! Your thought is lightning. Rend the solitude that withers you. Break the tower that contains your phantoms. Burst into flashes of Fire. In you there is the power to mold anew. Build blue kingdoms with the rectified "Magnesia".

4. Approach the majestic peaks of Purity.

The mountain air sings to exalt your toil. Remember, your destiny is to recognize yourself as eternal Fire. Discover the symbol of that Beauty which cannot decay.

5. Do not take these words as a simple outburst of poetry. This is not the time for idleness. Live the message of Accord with the philosophical Sulphur and reveal the miracle of Harmony in life. Space will respond to those who have learned to resonate with the chords of the Intellect of Love.

6. If you think, in your non-living, that I write to amuse you with ideal playthings, you are deluded.

Do not add other illusions to those that already hide the beauty of the Way from you. Upon the plane of Awakening every word is the harbinger of fruitful messages.

7. Perhaps your mind desires concepts, verbose dialectics or reasoning in order to convince and systematise, but all this is just to perpetuate the empirical ego.

Comprehend the darting dialogue made of flashes and of downpours. The idea rides upon rays of Fire.

Leave prolix and discursive thought and throw open the doors to pure Mercury.

The "Pathway of Fire" is not studied, but it is grasped through the lightning of intuition, through the comprehension of the heart and through identification of consciousness.

To "die" one does not need amusing conversations.

8. Instinct seeks relief, feelings seek an outlet, and the mind looks for simple systematic cognitions. The "Pathway of Fire" does not live on mental representations or *conceive* Reality; it does not offer toys to the desiring ego, but it approaches the Philosophers' Gold with the vibration of transfiguring Fire.

Knowledge is a flash of lightning that rends the weeping mists: whoever closes his eyes cannot grasp the resolving whirlwind.

Ideas are also an impetus of sound: whoever closes his ears loses that harmonic that discloses the blue of space.

9. What is the use of becoming erudite about what you have been and what you will be? Learn to live what you are now. Light Our Fire and lift it up to the King's Crown.

10. Selective thought is becoming and process, it is time. Your solution does not dwell in temporality. To transcend selective thought means to strike down the tower of "salt", your phantom, your chains and the cause of your suffering.

11. My friend, discursive thought causes you to linger and leads you on to tiring uphill climbs.
Know that your dreaming ego needs only one thing: its epitaph.

12. Perhaps you need profane ideals. Perhaps you thirst for esoteric *cognitions* or for occult powers. Perhaps you need to exercise political and professional activism, but remember that one day or another you will come to the cross-roads and your individuality will have to be resolved.
Only then will you be able to awaken to the contemplation of Beauty, the Good and the indivisible One.

13. Perhaps all your life you have wandered from one esoteric circle or spiritual group to another; perhaps for a long time you have not spoken of anything but realization and freedom from incompleteness. Perhaps you have desperately sought to convince others of the goodness of ultimate Truth. Perhaps you have felt pleased with your indoctrinated memory. Perhaps your aspiration has been reduced to producing printed

matter. Remember however that the day will come when your wandering, flattering and vain ego will have to be faced only with the disrupting *bolt*.

14. Imagining has reduced you to slavery. Discernment will lead you on to the Pathway. The ceasing of thought will take you beyond the Pathway.

15. «That which you contemplate beyond the just and the unjust, beyond this created (world) and beyond the uncreated, beyond past and future, it is *That*»[1].

16. Many desire, a few want but only some dare *to be*. The "Pathway of Fire" is for the few, for some, for qualified Philosophers.

17. If you are in anguish you do not live the Accord. If you weep for the dead, you have not comprehended; if you are the prisoner of identification, you do not reveal the archetypal Beauty; if your eyes do not twinkle with Bliss, you do not burn with all-pervading Fire.

18. Between your empirical self and the universal, there is "death"; if you are unable to dare your past will restrain you; if you are unable to dare, *avidyā* (metaphysical igno-rance) will envelop you; if you are not solar, the Dragon will overwhelm you.

The "Pathway of Fire" is not for the fearful.

---

[1] *Kaṭha Upaniṣad*: I, II, 14, in, *Upaniṣad*, Edited by Raphael. Op. cit.

19. If they flatter you with vanity, wealth or power, close the doors of your Temple. This is no time for distraction. Night might come upon you.

20. Turn your gaze to me, spread your wings, abandon your pain and your phantoms which were so dear to you up to this moment. A new paean approaches, *daring* and *ardor* are the steps of ascesis.

21. Violence is for the weak, calmness for the strong. The universal is not for the weak. Take up the shield of Patience and conquer that Dignity which will allow you to break down the doors of the senses.

22. Are you weak? Come.
I shall dry your tears red with blood. I shall rebuild your Temple of Light with cornerstones. I shall wash your feet which are caked in mud. Be joyful, oh blessed one, and grasp the symbol of Beauty. My Fire will lift you off the ground.

23. Whoever Loves dares and whoever dares, wins. The revolution is not meant for those who live in torpor. Victory is not for the dubious; glory hovers over the daring.

24. Do not hesitate; doubt belongs to the destitute ego. The Fire of Eros will give you the certainty of the eternal. Knowledge will give you the wings to cross the abyss. I love the fearless who dart toward the Infinite.

25. Are you in lethargy? The thunder will soon shake you. But perhaps it will be too late for you to get up and cut through your passiveness and your indolence.

26. Strengthen your yearning for perfection, rejoice in the vision that the Pathway offers you, turn your pupils toward the peak, but remember not to linger: the powers of darkness might frighten you.

27. Many calamities scourge the earth. New sprouts shall be watered by the tears of our errors and fertilized with the waste of our corpses.

28. You called me. I have come and yet you close your heart. Along the Pathway, curiosity is the forger of pain and pretence attracts the sword of anguish.

29. If you love the Universal, then learn the art of dying while living.
   If you yearn for the eternal Fire then you must turn your back on the contingent.

30. Let the sensorial world play with its own toys. Do not linger: your maturity imposes a new rhythm, a new accord, a new music capable of pacifying your existence.

31. The cycle is drawing to the sunset and the Shepherd calls his fold to new pastures, to a new dawn. Do not be distracted, unclench your teeth and let go of the prey which is no longer for you. Make haste lest the darkness come upon you along the Way.

APPENDIX

The Preface to the Commentaries of Plato
by Marsilio Ficino[1]
Addressed to the Magnanimous
Lorenzo de' Medici

«Magnanimous Lorenzo, Wisdom born from Jove's head alone was with him from the beginning, fashioning all things. Like her father, she too gave birth to a daughter from her head alone, a daughter named Philosophy, who would delight in being with the sons of men.

So this is why in former times, men of true worth everywhere strove to attain her as she travelled through the different nations upon earth. Of all these men our Plato not only strove after her but was the first and only one to worship her fully. For in acknowledging her holiness, he was the first to wreathe her brow with the priestly[2] garland and to robe her in a gown worthy of the noble daughter of Minerva. Then he anointed her head, hands, and feet with fragrant perfumes. Finally, wherever the spirit of Philosophy trod, he strew her path with a colorful carpet of flowers. Such was, and still is, the appearance and apparel of this goddess walking within the precincts of Academy...[3]

[Philosophy] delights in encouraging all who want to learn and to live well to enter the Platonic Academy. In the gardens of the Academy poets will hear Apollo singing beneath the laurels. In the forecourt orators will behold Mercury declaiming. In the porch and hall lawyers and statesmen will listen to Jove himself as he ordains laws, pronounces justice, and governs empires. Finally, within the innermost sanctuary philosophers will recognise their Saturn as he contemplates the secrets of the heavens. So come here, I beseech you, all you who pursue the ways of liberation; come here, for here you will reach your journey's end and attain freedom of life.⁴»

The Goddess Philosophy described by Marsilio Ficino and appearing on the front cover, is still poised in every work of Raphael and acts as his "sacred initiatrix" who conducts the seeker from the "Lesser Mysteries" to the "Greater Mysteries". The symbols of Alchemy, Love, Beauty and Metaphysics, expressed in that bronze, can be intuited and grasped in the realizative paths propounded in *The Threefold Pathway of Fire* which can rightly be considered as Raphael's *Summa Philosofica*.

---

[1] Marsilio Ficino, under the auspices of Cosimo de' Medici, carried out in Florence, where he was born in 1433, his work as humanist philosopher. He translated from Greek into Latin the *Corpus Hermeticum* of Hermes Trismegistus, the Orphic Hymns, the *Works* of Plato and the *Enneads* of Plotinus. In 1462 he founded a *Platonic Academy* constituted by a fellowship of thinkers and lovers of Platonic philosophy of which he was the guiding mind.

[2] It should be remembered that in the *Symposium* (201d; 209e; 210a) Plato raises Diotima, "The woman of Mantinea", to the dignity of the initiatrix to the Mysteries of Love:
«About Eros, I will tell you what one day I heard from Diotima, a woman of Mantinea, who was knowledgeable about this and other things as well ...
"Up to this level in the Mysteries of Love, Socrates, perhaps you might have been able to initiate yourself. But I do not know if you would be capable of attaining the perfect and contemplative doctrines to which, if one proceeds rightly, those ones expounded so far are but preparatory ones. I shall, therefore, expound them to you myself, she said, and will not fail to do my very best. You try and follow me, if you can"».

[3] The Platonic Academy was founded in Athens in 387 b.c. by Plato himself and was shut down by Justinian in 529 a.d.

[4] In, *Gardens on Philosophy*, Ficino on Plato, Translation by Arthur Farndell, Shepheard-Walwyn (Publishers) Ltd, London. (Minor revisions added).

RAPHAEL
Unity of Tradition

Having attained a synthesis of Knowledge (with which eclecticism or syncretism are not to be associated), Raphael aims at "presenting" the Universal Tradition in its many Eastern and Western expressions. He has spent a substantial number of years writing and publishing books on spiritual experience and his works include commentaries on the *Qabbālāh*, Hermetism and Alchemy. He has also commented on and compared the Orphic Tradition with the works of Plato, Parmenides and Plotinus. Furthermore, Raphael is the author of several books on the pathway of non-duality (*Advaita*), which he has translated from the original Sanskrit, offering commentaries on a number of key Vedantic texts.

With reference to Platonism, Raphael has highlighted the fact that, if we were to draw a parallel between Śaṅkara's *Advaita Vedānta* and a Traditional Western Philosophical Vision, we could refer to the Vision presented by Plato. Drawing such a parallel does not imply a search for reciprocal influences, but rather it points to something of paramount importance: a sole Truth, inherent in the doctrines and teachings of several great thinkers, who although far apart in time and space, have reached similar and in some cases even identical conclusions.

One notices how Raphael's writes from a metaphysical perspective in order to manifest and underscore the Unity of Tradition, under the metaphysical perspective. This does not mean that he is in opposition to a dualistic perspective, or to the various religious faiths, or "points of view".

A true embodied metaphysical Vision cannot be opposed to anything. What is important for Raphael is the unveiling, through living and being, of that level of Truth which one has been able to contemplate.

Writing in the light of the Unity of Tradition Raphael's works present, calling on the reader's intuition, precise points of correspondence between Eastern and Western Teachings. These points of reference are useful for those who want to approach a comparative doctrinal study and to enter the spirit of the Unity of Teaching.

For those who follow either an Eastern or a Western traditional line these correspondences help us comprehend how the *Philosophia Perennis* (Universal Tradition), which has no history and has not been formulated by human minds as such, «comprehends universal truths that do not belong to any people or any age». It is only for lack of "comprehension" or of "synthetic vision" that one particular Branch is considered the only reliable one. Such a position can but lead to opposition and fanaticism. What can degenerate the Doctrine is either a sentimental, fanatical devotion or condescending intellectualism, which is critical and sterile, dogmatic and separative.

In Raphael's words: «For those of us who aim at Realization, our task is to get to the essence of every Doctrine, because we know that just as Truth is one, so Tradition is one even if, just like Truth, Tradition may be viewed from a plurality of apparently different points of view. We must abandon all disquisitions concerning the phenomenal process of becoming, and move onto the plane of Being. In other words: we must have a Philosophy of Being as the foundation of our search and of our realization»[1].

Raphael interprets spiritual practice as a "Path of Fire". Here is what he writes: «...The "Path of Fire" is the pathway each disciple follows in all branches of Tradition; it is the Way of Return. Therefore, it is not the particular teaching of an individual nor a path parallel to the one and only Main Road... After all, every

---

[1] See, Raphael, *Tat tvam asi*, That thou art, Aurea Vidyā, New York.

disciple follows his own "Path of Fire", no matter which Branch of Tradition he belongs to».

In Raphael's view, what is important is to express through living and being the truth that one has been able to contemplate. Thus, for each being, one's expression of thought and action must be coherent and in agreement with one's own specific *dharma*.

After more than thirty-five years of teaching, both oral and written, Raphael is now dedicating himself only to those people who wish to be "doers" rather than "sayers", according to St. Paul's expression.

Raphael is connected with the *maṭha* founded by *Śrī Ādi* Śaṅkara at Śṛṅgeri and Kāñcipuram as well as with the Rāmaṇa Āśram at Tiruvannamalai.

Founder of the Āśram Vidyā Order, he now dedicates himself entirely to spiritual practice. He lives in a hermitage connected to the *āśram* and devotes himself completely to a vow of silence.

* * *

May Raphael's Consciousness, expression of Unity of Tradition, guide and illumine along this Opus all those who donate their *mens informalis* (non-formal mind) to the attainment of the highest known Realization.

PUBLICATIONS

Books by Raphael
published in English

At the Source of Life
Aurea Vidyā, New York

Beyond the illusion of the ego
Aurea Vidyā, New York

Essence and Purpose of Yoga
The Initiatory Pathways to the Transcendent
Element Books, Shaftesbury, Dorset, U.K.

Initiation into the Philosophy of Plato
Aurea Vidyā, New York

Orphism and the Initiatory Tradition
Aurea Vidyā, New York

Pathway of Fire, Initiation to the Kabbalah
S. Weiser, York Beach, Me., U.S.A.

The Pathway of Non-duality, Advaitavāda
Motilal Banarsidass, New Delhi

Tat tvam asi, That thou art,
The Path of Fire According to the Asparśavāda
Aurea Vidyā, New York

The Threefold Pathway of Fire
Aurea Vidyā, New York

Traditional Classics
in English

Śaṅkara, *Ātmabodha**, Self-knowledge.
Aurea Vidyā , New York

Bhagavadgītā, The Celestial Song*.
Aurea Vidyā, New York

Śaṅkara, *Drigdriśyaviveka**, Discernment between *ātman* and non-*ātman*. Aurea Vidyā, New York

Gauḍapāda, *Māṇḍūkyakārikā**, The Māṇḍūkya Upaniṣad with the verses-*kārikā* of Gauḍapāda and Commentary by Raphael.
Aurea Vidyā, New York

Parmenides, *On the Order of Nature*, Περί φύσεως**, For a Philosophical Ascesis. Aurea Vidyā, New York

Śaṅkara, *Vivekacūḍāmaṇi**, The Crest-jewel of Discernment.
Aurea Vidyā, New York

Forthcoming Publications
in English

Patañjali, *The Regal Way to Realization**, Yogadarśana

Śaṅkara, *Aparokṣānubhūti**, Self-realization

Bādarāyaṇa, *Brahmasūtra**

Five Upaniṣad*, Īśa, Kaivalya, Sarvasāra, Amṛtabindu, Atharvaśira

Raphael, *Pathway of Fire*, Initiation to the Kabbalah

* Translated from the Sanskrit, and Commented, by Raphael
** Edited by Raphael

Aurea Vidyā is the Publishing House of the Parmenides Traditional Philosophy Foundation, a Not-for-Profit Organization whose purpose is to make Perennial Philosophy accessible.

The Foundation goes about its purpose in a number of ways: by publishing and distributing Traditional Philosophy texts with Aurea Vidyā, by offering individual and group encounters and by providing a Reading Room and daily Meditations at its Center.

* * *

Those readers who have an interest in Traditional Philosophy are welcome to contact the Foundation at: parmenides.foundationṣearthlink.net.

Printed in July 2021
by Rotomail Italia S.p.A., Vignate (MI) - Italy